TALES OUT OF THE SCHOOL LIBRARY

Developing Professional Dispositions

Gail Bush and Jami Biles Jones

Foreword by Theodore R. Sizer

LIBRARIES UNLIMITED

AN IMPRINT OF ABC-CLIO, LLC
Santa Barbara, California • Denver, Colorado • Oxford, England

Library of Congress Cataloging-in-Publication Data

Bush, Gail.
  Tales out of the school library : developing professional dispositions / Gail Bush and Jami Biles Jones ; foreword
by Theodore R. Sizer.
     p. cm.
  Includes bibliographical references and index.
  ISBN 978-1-59158-832-0 (acid-free paper) — ISBN 978-1-59158-833-7 (ebook)
  1. School librarians—Psychology. 2. School librarians—Education (Continuing education) 3. School librari-
ans—In-service training. 4. Communication in education. 5. School librarians—Professional ethics. I. Jones, Jami
Biles. II. Title.
  Z682.4.S34B87 2010
  027.8—dc22   2009046648

14 13 12 11 10   1 2 3 4 5

This book is also available on the World Wide Web as an eBook.
Visit www.abc-clio.com for details.

ABC-CLIO, LLC
130 Cremona Drive, P.O. Box 1911
Santa Barbara, California 93116-1911

This book is printed on acid-free paper ∞
Manufactured in the United States of America

Dedicated with deep gratitude to Theodore R. Sizer,
educational visionary, reformer, and scholar,
with whom we had the pleasure of sharing
this collaborative writing process.

June 23, 1932–October 21, 2009

Contents

Horace's Story

During the early 1980s, with experience as the dean of the Harvard Graduate School of Education and as the headmaster of Phillips Academy in Andover, Massachusetts, under my belt, I decided to learn more about the U.S. high school. Through contacts, reading, and travel, I visited dozens of them, both in the United States and abroad, to learn both what made them work well and what challenged them.

Through the invention of suburban Franklin High School English teacher Horace Smith, a composite fictional character meant to represent a typical secondary school teacher, I was able to accommodate many variables across our country, including economic status, regional standards, and ethnic cultures. Horace is male and female, black and white, and Asian and Latino; he speaks for science teachers, coaches, counselors, mathematics teachers, and principals. If there could be an "Every High School U.S.A.," what I called Franklin High School would be that. The pressures that Horace faces in teaching 120 adolescents per year are felt by earnest teachers at all grade levels, who understand the impossibility of knowing each student well enough to respect the student as an individual, let alone to teach so that learning has any level of depth and meaning.

Many people who picked up the first book in the Horace trilogy (*Horace's Compromise; Horace's School; Horace's Hope*) had been frustrated by uninformed critics of both teachers and students. Despite the stereotypes, Horace was an intelligent and hard-working teacher who had been given an impossible job: too many students, too little time, with inadequate financial and no real moral support. My readers did not want to defend the *status quo* but, rather, get some ideas for constructive action.

In the first book, *Horace's Compromise: The Dilemma of the American High School,* I presented the situation as Horace experienced it. *Horace's Compromise* emerged out of a five-year-long, well-financed inquiry into adolescent education called "A Study of High Schools," which was sponsored by the National Association of Secondary School Principals and the Commission on Educational Issues of the National Association of Independent Schools. Our focus in the study was on the "triangle" of students, teachers, and the subjects of their study in both public and private schools. We held the belief that a society that is concerned about the strength and wisdom of its culture pays attention to its adolescents. When we tested that belief—how important knowledge and intellectual skills are transmitted—what we found was that in U.S. society the craft of teaching is singularly underrated; our traditional system is also trapped in a structure that leads to too many vast, anonymous, inflexible high schools. *Horace's Compromise* urged renewed public attention to the importance of teaching in high schools and to the complexity and subtlety of that craft. It drew attention to the conditions of work and the political and public respect that can be reasonably expected of educational professionals. Learning is a humane process, and teachers who have daily contact with youth are those best able to rise above the disadvantages of their workplace and set standards as models. *Horace's Compromise* was written to celebrate such work.

In the second book, *Horace's School: Redesigning the American High School,* published in 1992, Horace set about helping redesign his own high school so that good teachers could function at a high level. He believed that the Franklin High students knew how to play the high school game with exacting skill. They earned top grades, even in Advanced Placement classes, they participated in extracurriculars, including sports, yearbook, Student Council, and the like. But the high school, the community, the parents, and the students, comfortable with the *status quo,* perpetuated a shallow portrayal of a positive high school experience. Horace Smith, on the other hand, thought more deeply about the lack of serious thought and learning processes, about respectful skepticism, about intellectual curiosity. He worried that the game of high school that was being played so well at Franklin was doing a disservice to the very students he was responsible for teaching and that parents and "the system" had to understand this. Horace bemoaned the mindless machine that the U.S. high school had become—a thoughtless routine of pep rallies, quizzes, homecomings, and standardized exams. Horace realized that, by questioning one aspect of this "game," he was inherently questioning all; and yet he worried about the adults that his students would soon become and wondered how Franklin High School was preparing them to become independent critical thinkers.

At that defining moment, Horace had to decide whether to try to be a voice for reform or to find a way to tolerate the situation, as so many of his peers seemed to do with aplomb. So he took the plunge and chaired the Committee on Redesign that took a radically student-centered approach. The Committee included teachers, students, parents, a school board member, the principal, and an outside education consultant. Horace's not-so-hidden-agenda minimized the role of testing and maximized student work in the form of in-depth, problem-based independent projects that resulted in exhibitions and portfolios. In this way, Horace, ever the humanist—but still, alas, fictional—fought the good fight and improved his school.

Horace, and my readers, needed some hope! I sensed this when I traveled about the country introducing these ideas. Too many schools resisted change, and by the end of the century the ballooning growth of the state and national testing movements had made things even more difficult and complex. Many teachers and administrators were angry, frustrated, and thus ready to try something new. In this vein, in the last book in the trilogy, *Horace's Hope: What Works for the American High School,* Horace struggled with the understanding that the heart of schooling is found in relationships with students—only then do you have a chance of communicating ideas and inspiring intellectual curiosity. He also grasped that the student will have a place in the world in short order. Horace's hope resonated with those in the educational community who share the view that our students are remarkably resilient and that inching them toward a purposeful and fulfilling life beyond schooling is a worthy endeavor. Horace experienced support from unlikely community members, from complaining colleagues and parents bent on their children's elevated status at whatever cost. And so, Horace remains ever hopeful about the future of U.S. public education.

Through my books and in the Coalition of Essential Schools, founded in 1984, I tried to introduce the abundance of "Horaces"—including the "Horatias"—to each other. There is still much to do, not only in school restructuring, but also in improving teaching in every classroom and in every school library. Horace's message to school librarians would be to allow, indeed, to encourage, students to pursue and widen their own interests, and it is here that librarians can make a difference. The school library is the information conduit to the outside world. School librarians should make alliances with nearby libraries, not only for loaning books but for studying local and state governments. School librarians who are informed advocates for students are modeling adult behaviors in an authentic learning environment. Information skills transfer to academic libraries and public libraries and serve students as they independently search for authoritative information in pursuit of personal interests.

Above all, school librarians should love children, have inquiring minds, and respect books and information as one way to support those minds. As for technology, there should be a variety of tools, as different ways to perceive ideas usually intrigue children—especially with engaging emerging instructional technologies. Multiple perspectives on a given topic help develop divergent critical thinkers; every school library program, through the library collection, is responsible to represent a broad approach to thinking, including varieties of viewpoints and formats. The school librarian's role includes supporting teaching, using this vast array of resources, and integrating library and information skills across the curriculum. School librarians strive to encourage students to inquire (as children do naturally before "schooling" gets hold of them!) and then to act upon that inquiry. This deliberate process respects the students as informed citizens of a democratic society. The way we adults carry ourselves—how we deal with both vast amounts of information and relationships with others—will inevitably be watched by children. Indeed, my wife Nancy and I wrote more about that in our book *The Students Are Watching: Schools and the Moral Contract.*

Libraries have long played a big part in my life. I was a graduate student and then a professor and dean at Harvard; I ultimately extracted two books from the libraries there: *Secondary Schools at the Turn of the Century* and *The Age of the Academies.* Later, for a decade, Nancy and I were at Phillips Academy in Andover, Massachusetts; few schools have anything like their library. (When the British captured the town, they burned much of it, but not the Academy's book collection.) When we were there, we history teachers sent students into the collections; students serve as "librarian assistants."

Now, in my retirement, our little town's library is right next to the junior and senior high schools. Between them, they have a deep collection, and they offer services and programs to a variety of individuals and groups of all ages from morning until night. I'm not sure how many of those who enjoy our town library would put it this way, but, from my perspective, the life of the mind is celebrated there. This would make Horace—and his creator—very happy.

Theodore R. Sizer
Harvard, Massachusetts

REFERENCES

Sizer, T. R. 1964. *The age of academies.* New York: Columbia University.

Sizer, T. R. 1984. *Horace's compromise: The dilemma of the American high school.* Boston: Houghton Mifflin.

Sizer, T. R. 1992. *Horace's school: Redesigning the American high school.* Boston: Houghton Mifflin.

Sizer, T. R. 1996. *Horace's hope: What works for the American high school.* Boston: Houghton Mifflin.

Sizer, T. R. 1964. *Secondary schools at the turn of the century.* New Haven: Yale University.

Sizer, T. R., and N. Faust. 1999. *The students are watching: Schools and the moral contract.* Boston: Beacon Press.

Acknowledgments

Our mutual journey has engaged the generous encouragement of faculty colleagues, school library friends, and personal support systems. We are grateful to Junko Yokota and the staff of the Center for Teaching through Children's Books, Reading and Language Department colleagues, and inaugural Capstone Fellowship recipient Miriam Z. Rubinson at National-Louis University; and colleagues in the Library Science Department at Eastern Carolina University.

Our esteemed contributors Theodore R. Sizer and Nancy Faust Sizer, Gail K. Dickinson, and Carrie Gardner enrich the value of this book beyond what we could have accomplished alone. Our editor Sharon Coatney helped us continue to develop and refine our vision for this project, and the staff at Libraries Unlimited at ABC-CLIO have fostered it as both a landmark work and a learning experience, and we are deeply appreciative of their many efforts. And, last but most important, we humbly recognize that this endeavor was undertaken with the grace that may be granted only by the healthy gallery of family, friends, mentors, students, Maggie, and Mitzi.

Introduction

When we think about tales out of the school library and the tasks, responsibilities, and challenges of the school librarian, the concept of dispositions does not come readily to mind. On one hand, scheduling, lesson plans, class management, collection maintenance, communicating with teachers, administrators, and parents seem to be the bread and butter of the school librarian's every day pursuits. On the other hand, we have the vision to make a difference in the lives of our students, and we struggle to keep our aspirations high, with our feet stuck in the mud. And there we find ourselves facing an educational environment where dispositions have come to the forefront of the educator preparation field. Teacher education standards, learner standards, and, now, school librarian standards are focusing on dispositions of teaching and learning.

Listen to veterans of the education field, and they might dismiss the call for such a focus on dispositions. Thirty plus years ago, perhaps the need was not indicated. Societal decorum dictated behaviors in school that included dressing and talking appropriately, from both sides of the desk. Command of the English language was assumed, sentences were diagrammed, and respect for authority was *de rigueur*. There was a finite amount of information that was to be transmitted from teacher to student, and parental expectations were met when the report card was signed. Times have changed, educational mores have responded, and we find that professional dispositions are prominent in every aspect of preparing future educators and developing those who are already in the classroom and library.

Reflecting on that visionary quality, an abiding belief in the power of exemplary school librarians to make a difference in the lives of our students comes close to what some might consider, even beyond professional dispositions, to be a calling of sorts. In Howard Gardner's *Responsibility at Work: How Leading Professionals Act (or Don't Act) Responsibly* (2007), Mihaly Csikszentmihalyi and Jeanne Nakamura write in their chapter on "Creativity and Responsibility":

> Of all the forms of responsibility that . . . creative persons mention and demonstrate in their lives, perhaps the most important is their duty to do excellent work

as defined by the traditions and current standards of the particular activity in which they are engaged. To know how a person heeds this call is enormously important for society, because the excellence of the whole depends disproportionately on the energy and commitment of the few who, in all walks of life, want to change society for the better.

And therein lies the rub. School librarians are professional educators whose effectiveness is in large part dependent on our dispositions in light of the challenges we endure. Reflect upon those colleagues in whom you hold in the highest esteem and contemplate their most outstanding dispositions. Chances are that they will tell you that their level of success has been a journey that has taught them how to behave and respond in creative and caring ways. They will tell you that those dispositions that you identified have developed over time and continue to be fine-tuned with each school year that passes.

Csikszentmihalyi and Nakamura also suggest the following:

[T]he most important message that creative individuals have to convey . . . is a simple but vital one: there is no responsibility without care . . . care not only for the best examples of the past, but also for how best to perform their chosen medium right now—and how to improve and enrich the tradition. The call to excellence is a joyful calling. It is an ecstatic experience that benefits everyone—the creator who is lifted out of limited individual existence, and the community that is enriched by the quest for excellence.

Perhaps a strategic reader might surmise that the hidden agenda of this book is to move the field forward—one school librarian by one school librarian—through continuous reflection and development of our professional dispositions. Others might be more comforted to feel that the goal of this book is simply to introduce school librarians and school library graduate students to dispositions in an accessible and meaningful manner. Indeed, we strive to engage in response to each reader's experience with this text: to each reader, his or her book.

The chapter on dispositions illuminates the concept more fully and the reasons behind this new attention toward our professional approach. The content topics are those that are most prominent in school library environments, and the progression of the chapters follows a chronological school year from fall through summer. It also follows the dispositional development of three fictionalized school librarians. Elementary school librarian Lisa B. Taylor, middle school librarian Reggie G. Lorenz, and high school librarian Donna M. Janceski are amalgams of the many school librarians the authors have met across the country in schools and at professional development workshops and conferences. The notion of the amalgam of an educator to guide the reader's thinking through the book comes from Theodore R. Sizer and his fictionalized nonfiction trilogy protagonist, Horace Smith, a teacher at Franklin High School, based on the hundreds of teachers Dr. Sizer met in his travels as an education scholar and reformer. Learn more about Theodore R. Sizer and Horace Smith in the foreword to this book.

Historically there have been other case studies books in the school library field, and it is hoped that there will be more to come (a favorite is the 1989 *Case Studies in Managing School Library Media Centers* by Daniel Callison and Jacqueline Morris). Many current professional books in our field include brief tales as discussion prompts. The major difference with the approach in this book is that the reader is invited to make connections with the school librarians who are living through identifiable experiences in their school environments that help us reflect upon our own approach and response to situations and tales. We are able to see Lisa, Reggie, and Donna journey through a school year, and we can approximate the change and growth of dispositions over time. And yet the reader will empathize with their continuing struggles. Meet your tour guides for *Tales Out of the School Library: Developing Professional Dispositions* in the prologue that follows this introduction, and be sure to follow them all the way through to the epilogue.

Each chapter is presented in the following pattern:

- Introductory paragraph
- Tales featuring Lisa, Reggie, or Donna
- LET'S DISCUSS: Conversational discussion covering the essentials of each topic
- QUESTIONS AND ANSWERS: Key questions and answers—natural "yes, but . . ." afterthoughts
- READ MORE ABOUT: Selected annotated bibliography
- CONNECT TO 21ST-CENTURY LEARNERS: Connections to *AASL Standards: Dispositions in Action* (2007) highlighted for each topic
- DISPOSITIONAL PROMPTS: Designed for reflection and discussion in networking groups, classes, workshops, professional development activities or for self-reflection

In addition to the content mentioned previously, the reader is treated to quotes from literature for all ages, words of wisdom and folly. It is our intent to educate, entertain, and inspire our trusted readers. It is our hope that our readers cum colleagues will reflect on their professional dispositions; on their responsibilities to their students, to themselves, and to our field as a community; and will be moved to take individually meaningful and purposeful steps to improve their practice for their own enrichment and, ultimately, to make a difference for all our learners.

REFERENCES

AASL. 2007. *Standards for the 21st-century learner.* Chicago: American Library Association.

Callison, D., and J. Morris. 1988. *Case studies in managing school library media centers.* Phoenix, AZ: Oryx Press.

Csikszentmihaly, M., and J. Nakamura. 2007. Creativity and responsibility. In *Responsibility at work: How leading professionals act (or don't act) responsibly,* ed. by Howard Gardner, 64–80. San Francisco: Jossey-Bass.

Prologue

The school year is just getting started. School librarians around the country have spent time this past summer reading new picture books or young adult novels; attending professional development workshops; visiting virtual museums; and enjoying their family and friends, so that they will be refreshed and ready for a new year of rewarding challenges and a few happy surprises sprinkled here and there.

Three of those school librarians are Lisa Taylor, Reggie Lorenz, and Donna Janceski, colleagues you might have met in your graduate classes, at a library networking meeting, or professional development workshop. Lisa is starting her third year in an elementary school, Reggie is moving into the library from his district technology department, and Donna is in her sixth year as school librarian, after teaching high school language arts for ten years. Reading about their backgrounds will give you added insight into their perspectives as you progress through the school year with them. Each librarian is included in every section of the book; the Epilogue that follows the body of the book gives you an opportunity to end your journey with your new found friends.

Lisa B. Taylor spent five years in retail and kept thinking that she really wanted to be teaching science, because that is her passion. Lisa saved her money, quit her job at the bookstore, earned a master's in teaching (MAT) and spent one agonizing year in the classroom. Painfully realizing it was not for her, Lisa moved from middle school science to a school library in hopes of staying in the school environment but with a different twist. In order to find a job as a school librarian, Lisa had to move to an elementary school, which concerned her.

Lisa is in her late twenties, single, African American, and has an apartment in the city that she adores. She was a department manager in a large bookstore before completing an MAT. Her undergraduate degree was in biology; she was good in science in high school and has a healthy intellectual curiosity about the world; she minored in business. At first, Lisa thought about teaching high school because she wanted to teach science at a level where students could really understand it, but then she had to be honest with herself, Lisa was afraid of teaching teenagers in the high school. She acclimated to the idea of teaching at the middle school level because that is such a critical age, a turning point for many kids. Her MAT prepared her for teaching middle school science, but she is certified for kindergarten through eighth grade. Lisa felt fine with the seventh and eighth grade students in her classes with the classroom door shut but did not like the "middle school philosophy"; she understood that it must work if the teachers get along, but Lisa did not feel that her colleagues respected the struggling students, and that made her not respect her colleagues. Lisa decided to move into the library—mostly because of the technology but also because she likes the research side of science and feels that she could bring that scientific inquiry into other contexts.

Although Lisa had worked at a bookstore, she was still surprised that she liked her children's and adolescent literature courses in graduate school; her favorite genres are science fiction and fantasy, but she likes nonfiction most of all. Lisa played soccer until junior year of high school; she likes bike riding, and she used to like her rollerblades. Lisa still has close friends from the bookstore; she likes to go to superhero movies that have lots of technical effects. Lisa enjoys going to big family events and is close with her brother's family, especially his wife, who is a little older than Lisa, and she loves their baby and their dog. Lisa cannot have pets in her apartment. Lisa has a vacation planned—to go to Costa Rica with a few friends to go on an eco-trip. She feels engaged in the world somehow when she can combine travel with her interest in science. Also, Lisa's Spanish is pretty fair, and she likes to work on improving it, especially to help with families whose first language is Spanish. Lisa likes languages in general; she just thinks they are fascinating, especially the whole idea of how they developed.

Lisa has had a few boyfriends, nothing steady yet, but she is really happy not to be in an unhappy relationship—some of those boyfriends went sour before they went away—she is just fine, thank you very much. Lisa feels like she has time, is in no hurry to rush into anything. She likes some of her friends' relationships with their boyfriends and husbands, some not so much. Lisa has a male friend from college, William, and, well, who knows, they are just friends, date other people, but love to hang out together.

Reggie G. Lorenz held a technology position for seven years and was persuaded to accept the library position in the middle school if he wanted to stay in the district. Reggie is easy-going, likeable, in his early thirties but looks much younger, Filipino American, he comes from a close family, with three older sisters who all are married and two of whom have families. Reggie is single but has a group of friends from his church and his softball team. Reggie has an undergraduate degree in computer science; he started out at the community college and finished at the local university. In order to get his certification in instructional technology, he attended a local college of education. Recently, his district gave him the option of going into the library when his position was cut—there used to be seven members in the K–12 district technology department—now only one person is handling all the technology, and he had more seniority in the district than Reggie. He thinks that this is fine; Reggie loves doing research using the Internet and does not think that the teachers do a good job using technology or online content in their teaching.

When Reggie worked in the district technology department, he taught lots of professional development. He is extremely patient but would then get frustrated when the same teachers who attended the workshops did not integrate what they learned from him into their teaching. Reggie is taking classes to receive his endorsement in school libraries; he has a three-year waiver to complete his credit hours, even though his district is letting him have the library media specialist position; he does not need to take any additional technology courses. He is grateful, because he wants to stay in this consolidated district. Reggie helps out coaching the high school tennis team and thinks about sponsoring a middle school technology club. Reggie lives in an apartment complex not too far from the district or his parents. Reggie likes to play video games, he does not read much, but he likes to sketch, doodle really, and is mildly interested in the new graphic novel craze. Reggie has a great smile and dry sense of humor, and the students like him but don't always respect his authority as much as he would like. He dates but nothing serious yet. Reggie dated a teacher in the district two years ago but decided that was not a good idea for him. He mostly goes out with his friends in groups and is almost ready to meet someone—but this would not be a great time—maybe after the courses are finished. Reggie is interested in traveling and has gone on a few mission trips with his church group. He especially likes to visit national parks and maybe wants to try to visit all of them in his lifetime. Outside of the United States, so far he has traveled only to the Philippines and Mexico but wants to think about a trip next summer if he could fit it in between graduate classes.

Donna M. Janceski is a 10-year veteran teacher who moved into the library in her high school six years ago. A former English teacher, Donna taught mostly honors and Advanced Placement, with a few regular classes once in a while. Donna Marie is of Italian ancestry, and her husband Ray is a Czech American. Donna likes to think that their two daughters are "real Americans" because of the mix of cultures. Donna stayed home for a just a few years with the girls. Elizabeth is a senior at the high school, and Gwen is a sophomore in college. Both of Donna's daughters are swimmers, were in the National Honors Society, and are serious students. Gwen is attending a state university that is a four-hour drive from home. Donna and Ray live in one of the moderately affluent communities that feed into the high school.

Donna considers herself to be open-minded, fair, and feels very patriotic and that, in a sense, it is her duty to help build a strong society by serving her students—with high standards for their learning and their decorum. When her daughters want something, they have learned to ask Dad, but Donna knows that they understand that by her refusals, she is trying to help them become successful women. Donna likes to watch movies with her daughters, she used to knit, she likes to try new recipes, and she does a very little bit of gardening during the summer. Her favorite color is turquoise, and her favorite author is Jodi Picoult. And Donna loves Oprah but does not agree with many of her book club selections.

Donna struggled with her decision to leave the classroom, because she did not want to lose the close relationship that English teachers make with their students. But she just kept looking ahead to the next 20-plus years and decided that if she did not want to continue teaching honors English for the rest of her career, after 10 years in the classroom, it was the best time to make a change. When she was teaching, she had lots of ideas to improve the library and she knew the teachers so well that she thought that they would like it if she was in the library. She is not terribly interested in the technology side of things, but there is a good technology teacher, so she has never worried about that. And, to be honest, she does not miss all the grading that English teachers do, which she does not think *anyone* understands. So the library seemed like a great fit for her. She was an education major in college, with a literature minor. Donna likes to keep up on current events but likes to know more about local politics than what is happening around the world. She is hoping that her daughters will stay close to home to raise their families when the time comes, but that is still a few years off. For now, Donna and Ray have a nine-year-old mixed breed dog (they think that there is some spaniel there) named Charley (á la Steinbeck); they really like to take long walks with Charley in the state park on weekends. Donna and Ray take family trips to visit relatives; sometimes they rent cottages with their siblings and their daughters and go fishing, swimming, etc. Donna is looking forward to traveling after they retire. She wants to start by going to London, Rome, and Prague, and then the rest of Europe sounds grand. But that too is a long way off.

Lisa, Reggie, and Donna have very full lives, just like school librarians everywhere. Their professional positions each present a myriad of situations that require countless daily decisions. How they choose to handle a selection of colleagues, students, opportunities, and mishaps may be found in the tales that accompany the following chapters. Read, reflect, and repeat. And, finally, be sure to meet up with Lisa, Reggie, and Donna in the Epilogue to see how they are each finding their way on this wild and wondrous journey that we all share.

Chapter One

Dispositions

As former students, we recognize that some teachers are quite remarkable—they have that special "something" that sets them apart from others who are . . . well . . . not quite so inspiring. Students flourish under the tutelage of remarkable teachers, but they stagnate in the presence of less talented ones. Even if you cannot quite put your finger on these qualities, you know they exist and are the difference between a truly amazing educational experience and one that is "ho hum." You are right to suspect that remarkable teachers are different, and it has to do with personal and professional behaviors known as dispositions.

In the mid-1990s, Vivienne Collinson (1996) of the University of Maryland's College of Education asked the most effective elementary, middle, and high school teachers she knew the following question: "What makes an exemplary teacher exemplary?" She discovered that the amazing teachers (the kind we all want for our children) excel in three areas: professional knowledge about the subject matter, curriculum, and pedagogy; interpersonal knowledge to form positive relationships with students, the educational community, and the local community; and intrapersonal knowledge that focuses on the personal qualities of reflection, ethics, and dispositions.

> Peak performers develop powerful images of the behavior that will lead to the desired results. They see in their mind's eye the result they want, and the actions leading to it.
>
> Charles Garfield, computer scientist, psychologist, author, and athlete

A decade later, Kathleen Cushman (2006), a Coalition of Essential Schools researcher, asked 65 *students* to describe the qualities of the teacher they most wanted. Students told Cushman they want engaging classes taught by teachers who like and care about the material they teach, treat their students as smart and capable of challenging work, and are respectful of them, caring, and trustworthy. Although the audiences were different, Collinson's and Cushman's findings are remarkably similar. In a nutshell, exemplary teachers and high school students agree that students flourish when teachers possess the personal and professional dispositions to understand and be enthused by the subject matter they teach, can communicate and relate to students, and create a caring and nurturing environment. As educators, each of us has observed colleagues who relate well to students and whose students want to be in their presence, are enthusiastic about the subject they teach, and effortlessly create a learning environment in which students blossom. But what are these dispositions *exactly*?

> Behavior is what a man does, not what he thinks, feels, or believes.
>
> Anonymous

In the mid-1980s, Lilian G. Katz, early childhood education scholar and leading expert on this topic, and colleague James Raths described dispositions as behaviors with the following characteristics:

- Observable
- Exhibited frequently
- "Habits of mind"
- Consciously and voluntarily applied
- Intentionally oriented to broad goals (Katz and Raths 1986, 7)

Some might ask why it is not enough to be credentialed by your state's educational agency. After all, is it unfair to ask teachers to exhibit certain behaviors that are nebulous to describe and untested? The concept of dispositions raises concerns because it seems subjective and difficult to assess, but it is important to remember that dispositions are *behavioral choices*—they are observable behaviors that are consciously and voluntarily applied to specific situations. However, concerns continue and fall into three categories:

1. The *terminology* of dispositions. Words such as attitudes, traits, personality characteristics, values, beliefs, affective characteristics, habits, theories, perceptions, and sense of efficacy are often used synonymously with dispositions, although their meaning is not the same. For instance, *traits* are inborn characteristics, such as height, eye color, or introversion/extroversion; *attitudes* are judgments regarding likes and dislikes, usually measured with scales; and *habits* are learned behaviors, displayed routinely without forethought, such as fastening one's seat belt before driving off.
2. The *teaching* of dispositions. How are dispositions taught and who teaches these to educators and school librarians?
3. The *identification* and *assessment* of dispositions. Who determines which dispositions are important? How are dispositions assessed? Who does this assessing? What happens if an individual is lacking a particular disposition (or two) that is deemed important? Or if he or she is missing the mark by a wide margin? Will the educator or school librarian be punished by losing his or her job? It is important to restate that dispositions are behavioral *choice*s within one's reach to acquire and nurture if so motivated.

The National Council for the Accreditation of Teacher Education (NCATE) describes dispositions as the "professional attitudes, values, and beliefs demonstrated through both verbal and non-verbal behaviors as educators interact with students, families, colleagues, and communities" that can be observed and assessed. NCATE explicitly recognizes only two dispositions—fairness and the belief that all students can learn, although we know there are other dispositions necessary for educators.

Even though the National Board of Professional Teaching Standards (NBPTS) does not define dispositions, it does expect that accomplished teachers be able to employ the necessary "skills, capacities, and dispositions" embedded in the *Five Core Propositions*. These are (1) dedication to student learning, (2) understanding the subject and being able to teach it to students, (3) management and monitoring of student learning, (4) thinking systematically about their practice and learning from experiences, and (5) participating in learning communities. Within each of these propositions, the NBPTS further delineates the behaviors of accomplished teachers. The Five Core Propositions are found at http://www.nbpts.org/the_standards/ the_five_core_propositio.

Perhaps the most robust dispositional model for us is the *Standards of the Interstate New Teacher Assessment and Consortium* (INTASC). The operating premise of INTASC is that an effective teacher must be able to integrate content knowledge with pedagogical understanding and dispositions to ensure that all students learn and perform at high levels. The 10 core principles (in italics) and the dispositions attached to each are described in more detail by Daniel T. Holm in *The Passion of Teaching: Dispositions in the Schools* (2005, 112–113):

1. *Content knowledge* dispositions are associated with a teacher's enthusiasm for the discipline and lifelong learning, an understanding to pursue new knowledge, and an appreciation of multiple perspectives.
2. *Development* dispositions are associated with respect of a student's strengths and talents.
3. *Individual differences* dispositions are associated with a teacher's belief that all children can be successful learners.
4. *Instruction for diverse learners* dispositions are associated with valuing the varied abilities that students bring to the classroom and the willingness to adapt instruction to meet the diverse needs of all students.
5. *Learning environment* dispositions are associated with the teacher organizing the classroom in such a way that all students can be successful in a positive instructional climate.
6. *Communication with students* dispositions are associated with the fostering of a positive classroom environment that values self-expression.
7. *Instructional planning* dispositions are associated with short- and long-term planning, while realizing that plans are flexible, based on the needs of students.
8. *Assessment* dispositions are associated with ongoing process of monitoring a student's strengths and areas for improvement.
9. *Reflective practice* dispositions are associated with a teacher who seeks out help, as well as a teacher who is willing to modify his or her instructional plans to better meet the needs of students.
10. *Communication with community* dispositions are associated with valuing the importance of all aspects of a student's life experiences.

An excellent resource for learning about the concept of dispositions is *Teacher Dispositions: Building a Teacher Education Framework of Moral Standards,* edited by Hugh Sockett. This slim volume conceptualizes dispositions, which can be difficult to grasp. Sockett (2006) describes dispositions as "the professional virtues, qualities, and habits of mind and behavior held and developed by teachers on the basis of their knowledge, understanding, and commitments to students, families, their colleagues, and communities" (23). It is worth struggling with the concept of dispositions because it is these that identify the values and actions of

> We must become the change we want to see.
>
> Mahatma Gandhi, Indian political leader,
> 1869–1948

exemplary school librarians and the "development of dispositions of character, intellect, and caring are the core of professional teaching" (Sockett 2006, 21).

Although the *AASL Standards for the 21st-Century Learner,* which comprise the four learning strands of skills, dispositions in action, responsibilities, and self-assessment strategies, are intended to guide the development of students, they might also serve to inform the behaviors of exemplary school librarians because **dispositions are best acquired, taught, and caught through modeling**.

In a sense, the dispositions in action of these standards become the *de facto* dispositions for school librarians, because, in the words of NBPTS, accomplished teachers are "models of educated persons, exemplifying the virtues they inspire in students" (NBPTS). To model these dispositions in action successfully for students, school librarians must have acquired them first. The student dispositions standardized by the American Association of School Librarians (AASL) are the following:

- Display initiative, engagement, emotional resilience, persistence, curiosity.
- Demonstrate confidence, self-direction, creativity, adaptability, flexibility, personal productivity, leadership, teamwork, motivation.
- Maintain (and employ) a critical stance, openness to new ideas.
- Use both divergent and convergent thinking.
- Have (and show) an appreciation for social responsibility (see Appendix for Dispositions in Actions).

Now that you understand the concept of dispositions and those of exemplary classroom teachers, as well as school librarians, the next step is to assess your dispositional strengths and weaknesses informally. The dispositions previously mentioned are the "gold standard" to which we strive. Dispositions are not meant to keep individuals from becoming school librarians, but rather to inform our practice as we become the most effective

> To change a habit, make a conscious decision and then act out the new behavior.
>
> Maxwell Maltz, motivational author,
> 1927–2003

school librarians possible. A discussion about dispositions can cause educators to feel uncomfortable because of their fear of not measuring up. An informal assessment of your dispositions will most likely reveal that you are solid in some but have room for growth in others. Although it is true that the best teachers share a cluster of dispositions, it is also true that dispositions are within everyone's grasp if they *want* to grow and develop in these areas.

So what happens if, after assessing and reflecting on your dispositions, a few of the "gold standard" dispositions are missing or need strengthening? Be assured that none of us has all these dispositions; those we have fall in the spectrum from "accomplished" to "needs improvement."

Two researchers with Project Zero at Harvard's Graduate School of Education, Shari Tishman and David Perkins, have identified three essential components of dispositional behavior that can be used as we reflect on, assess, and develop dispositions. Let us consider fairness, one of two dispositions that NCATE explicitly recognizes, and how we would apply

Tishman and Perkins's three essential components of dispositional behavior to act fairly. The first component is *sensitivity* to recognize the need for a particular disposition—it is having your antennae up to notice opportunities to act in certain ways that you know will improve the learning environment for children. You are *sensitive* to using the disposition of fairness in situations in which fairness is recognized as the most appropriate action at that time.

The second component is to have the *inclination* to want to act in certain ways that you know will improve the learning environment for children. For a behavior to be a disposition, it must be put into action. According to the *Random House College Dictionary* that sits on my bookshelf, a skill is the "ability to do something well, arising from talent, training, or practice." However, one can be skilled without being inclined or disposed to use the skill. Let us use reading to explain the difference between a skill and a disposition. A student can be a skilled reader and perform well on comprehension tests, but this does not ensure that he or she will *frequently* and *voluntarily* engage with reading—in other words, be inclined to exhibit the disposition of reading.

The third component is to have the *follow-through knowledge* that will allow you to "seize the moment successfully" in order to act in certain ways that you know will improve the learning environment for children. Participating in professional development, reading professional literature, and reflecting on practice are ways to gain follow-through knowledge.

> Human behavior flows from three main sources: desire, emotion, and knowledge.
> Plato, Greek philosopher, 428 BC–348 BC

When it comes to dispositions, the choice is yours to act in certain ways, or not. If you are unwilling (not *inclined*) to acquire the dispositions identified in the NCATE, INTESC, and AASL standards and NBPTS core principles, perhaps you want to consider if this profession is a good fit for you.

To help students acquire and exhibit the dispositions in action described in the *AASL Standards for the 21st-Century Learner* we must first have acquired and exhibited these ourselves. One model for teaching and modeling dispositions for students is presented by Sergiovanni (1992):

- Say it. Define and communicate the disposition.
- Model it. Act on the disposition.
- Organize for it. Put it into resources, dialogues, personal contact.
- Support it. Provide resources to promote core values.
- Enforce it. Embody core values in personal assessments.
- Express it. Tell people why it is important—repeatedly (73).

A second way for students to acquire dispositions (and for us to teach them) is through children's literature. Let us consider the 1952 classic *Charlotte's Web* by E. B. White—and how the interaction between Charlotte and Wilbur is helpful to students—to acquire two AASL *Dispositions in Action*, 1.2.6 and 1.2.7, about persistence, a quality of continuing steadily or firmly in some state, purpose, or course of action, which is important to searching and obtaining information. Persistence is one disposition modeled throughout *Charlotte's Web,* but in Chapter Nine of this book, Wilbur boasts that he is able to spin a spider web because it doesn't look so difficult to him after all. Charlotte directs Wilbur to spin a web by "hurling yourself into space, and let out a dragline as you go down!" (56). As expected, the first attempt fails, but

Wilbur tries again by enlisting the assistance of Templeton the rat, who provides a piece of string that is tied to Wilbur's tail. Charlotte "was proud to see that he was not a quitter and was willing to try again to spin a web" (58). Whenever the need to persist arises in the classroom, the image of Wilbur spinning a web provides the model for students, because dispositions are best acquired, taught, and caught through modeling—even if the model is Wilbur the pig!

REFERENCES

Collinson, V. 1996, July. *Becoming an exemplary teacher: Integrating professional, interpersonal, and intrapersonal knowledge.* Paper presented at the annual meeting of the Japan-United States Teacher Education Consortium, Naruto, Japan. http://eric.ed.gov/ERICDocs/data/ericdocs2sql/content_storage_01/0000019b/80/14/c6/2f.pdf.

Cushman, K. 2006. Help us care enough to learn. *Educational Leadership* 63(5): 35–37.

Katz, L., and J. Raths. 1986, July. *Dispositional goals for teacher education: Problems of identification and assessment.* Paper presented at the World Assembly of the International Council on Education for Teaching, Kinston, Jamaica. http://eric.ed.gov/ERICDocs/data/ericdocs2sql/content_storage_01/0000019b/80/32/26/62.pdf.

Sergiovanni, T. 1992. *Moral leadership: Getting to the heart of school improvement.* San Francisco: Jossey-Bass.

Sockett, H. 2006. Character, rules, and relations. In *Teacher dispositions: Building a teacher education framework of moral standards,* ed. by Hugh Sockett, 9–25. Washington, DC: AACTE Publications.

STANDARDS CITED

American Association of School Librarians. *Standards for the 21st-Century Learner.* http://www.ala.org/ala/mgrps/divs/aasl/aaslproftools/learningstandards/AASL_Learning_Standards_2007.pdf.

American Library Association. American Association of School Librarians. *ALA/AASL Standards for Initial Programs for School Library Media Specialist Preparation.* http://www.ncate.org/documents/ProgramStandards/ala%202001.pdf.

Council of Chief State School Officers. *Interstate New Teacher Assessment and Support Consortium Core Standards.* http://resources.css.edu/academics/EDU/undergrad/forms/0405/INTASCStandards&EDUDispositionsAlignment.pdf.

National Board for Professional Teaching Standards. *What Teachers Should Know and Be Able to Do.* http://www.nbpts.org/UserFiles/File/what_teachers.pdf.

READ MORE ABOUT DISPOSITIONS

Jones, J., and G. Bush. 2009. What defines an exemplary school librarian? An exploration of professional dispositions. *Library Media Connection* 27(6): 10–12.

Jones and Bush describe dispositions (and what they are not) and provide guidance for acquiring and developing them. Examples of dispositions of school librarians are culled from NCATE, INTASC, and other standards.

Diez, M. E., and J. Raths, eds. 2007. *Dispositions in teacher education*. Charlotte, NC: IAP-Information Age Publishing.

The 11 chapters accumulated in this work provide a multifaceted approach to understanding a confusing topic—the theoretical dispositions in teacher education. John Raths is a foremost contributor on this topic and has written extensively with another leading expert, Lilian G. Katz.

Smith, R. L., D. Skarbek, and J. Hurst, eds. 2005. *The passion of teaching: Dispositions in the schools*. Lanham, MD: Scarecrow Education.

This book provides an overview of the historical and definitional perspectives of dispositions, as well as the contemporary views of dispositions. The two books, read together, will provide school librarians with a solid base from which to understand the importance of dispositions during a time of high stakes testing.

Sockett, H., ed. 2006. *Teacher dispositions: Building a teacher education framework of moral standards*. Washington, DC: AACTE Publications.

One of the best books for explaining the moral dimensions of teaching and the concept of dispositions is a slim volume composed of three chapters, Three prestigious faculty members contributed to this fascinating book.

Stripling, B. 2008. Dispositions: Getting beyond "Whatever." *School Library Media Activities Monthly* 25, 47–50.

Stripling urges school librarians to apply dispositions to counter students' indifference. She defines dispositions and places them within the context of the *AASL Standards for the 21st-Century Learner*.

Section One

Nuts and Bolts

Chapter Two

Instructional Strategies

Are we librarians or are we teachers? A resounding "yes." We have the benefit of straddling intertwining professional fields that serve learners regardless of age. In the school library, our primary responsibility is to students, but we also serve our teachers, administrators, parents, and community members. The manner in which we serve our patrons is in large part a teaching function. But when that tired question comes up about "being a teacher," it is often considered to mean a "classroom teacher," as opposed to having a strong teaching role in school libraries and, in fact, in any library position. Ours is a learning environment, and our role is a teaching role and then some.

REGGIE

I'm new here but not really. I know most of the teachers because I taught them all in the technology professional development workshops that the district offers and I would come around to fix things for them. Mostly everything I did was more hardware related. It is weird that the district brings in instructional programs and then teaches the teachers how to use them. There is just something backward there, it never seems to work very well except on rare occasion. But that was my old gig and now I am the media specialist in the Library Media Center at Thomas Jefferson Middle School and I am lost if I get too far away from the computers.

I am not too worried really. The LMC seems pretty independent of anything going on in the classrooms. The teachers teach and they use the LMC for the computers and for their students to check out books for book reports. I am not a reader but to me the books we have look OK. I know that I will need to order some new books eventually but there isn't a lot of money to spend anyway. Otherwise, I don't think that there is so much to do in the LMC. From what I have learned so far in my grad classes I am supposed to want to collaborate with teachers. I just don't see it that way. The teachers teach and I am in the LMC mostly making sure everything is in order for them. I don't see the problem with that. If they want me to do anything special I just figure that they will let me know.

I have my certificate by way of my instructional technology degree and I am comfortable teaching the teachers how to use the technology but that seems almost futile. Most teachers would rather use what they know. Even if they know how to use something they don't really understand how to use it to teach—especially when the students are more comfortable with the technology than they are. I think it makes middle school teachers feel uneasy because their authority is so important for maintaining control. We don't talk about discipline much in our classes but that is the real world. This year I will watch and think about what to do differently in the LMC when I understand my job better.

LET'S DISCUSS INSTRUCTIONAL STRATEGIES

At the risk of offending serious scholars of educational pedagogy, we find ourselves at the meeting of the Dewey boys, John and Melvil. In his seminal works in the pursuit of progressive education, John Dewey emphasizes the life of the child as the starting point for any learning experience. In *The Child and the Curriculum,* Dewey (1902/1990) implores educators to:

> Abandon the notion of subject-matter as something fixed and ready-made in itself, outside the child's experience; cease thinking of the child's experience as also something hard and fast; see it as something fluent, embryonic, vital; and we realize that the child and the curriculum are simply two limits which define a single process. Just as two points define a straight line, so the present standpoint of the child and the facts and truths of studies define instruction. It is continuous reconstruction, moving from the child's present experience out into that represented by the organized bodies of truth that we call studies. (189)

Realizing our teaching function in an independent learning environment provides us with opportunities to act on Dewey's admonition. We begin with the student in our heart and mind and progress from there. We are mandated to teach all children and provide equal access to the general curriculum; our collections support all children in their learning. Our best practices are those that engage students personally with the content and encourage connections to be made across and within disciplines; effective school library instructional strategies relate to our students as learners who come to the content with prior knowledge, experience, and curiosity. Learning is a personal, social, and generative process as knowledge is built from meaning. The school library is equipped both with the print collection to support learning and foster a love of reading and the technology to support social learning and the construction of learning communities.

Melvil Dewey created a classification and cataloging system that organizes the world's knowledge. All information has a place in the library. John Dewey posited that critical thinkers are essential for a democratic form of government, and toward that goal our schools need to challenge students to learn by doing. Active, authentic learning combines three elements: the learner, the society, and the body of knowledge.

> Listen to the mustn'ts, child. Listen to the don'ts. Listen to the shouldn'ts, the impossibles, the won'ts. Listen to the never haves, then listen close to me . . . Anything can happen, child. Anything can be.
>
> Shel Silverstein, American poet and author of children's books, 1930–1999

DOMAINS OF LEARNING

Curriculum models that promote best practices in learning vary in their focus on content, process, and outcomes. However, all models address three domains of learning that help structure instruction: cognitive, affective, and psychomotor.

The cognitive domain takes center stage in most formal learning environments. This is the domain of ideas, of knowing and thinking, of rational learning; it is populated by hierarchies and taxonomies of learning, of learning outcomes and behavioral objectives.

The affective domain is the domain of emotional learning, caring, and feeling. Emotional learning includes becoming aware through showing, responding by following, and developing attitudes by choosing. Our dispositions around teaching and learning reside within the affective domain.

The psychomotor domain is the physical world of learning where we manipulate learning through artifacts and detect errors through perception and sensory cues; prepare to act by assuming positions; and practice and demonstrate understanding.

> It is the supreme art of the teacher to awaken joy in creative expression and knowledge.
>
> Albert Einstein, German theoretical physicist and winner of the 1921 Nobel Prize in Physics, 1879–1955

The learning environment of the school library is poised and ready to welcome all learning materials, all domains of learning, and, most important, all students regardless of whether instruction is individual, small group, or the whole class. Our interdisciplinary approach and focus on inquiry learning provides our teachers with new perspectives on teaching the content of the grade-level curriculum. With such a wealth of opportunities, how do we know which strategies to employ in the school library?

Perhaps one approach will be to discuss overarching strategies, the type that we might discuss with teachers as we collaboratively plan for instruction. The specific instructional strategies might also be mentioned, or you might prefer to have a few handy techniques that you learn to use comfortably for many different disciplines and grade levels. In fact, utilizing similar strategies with various content areas helps students see both commonalities and distinctions.

COLLABORATIVE PLANNING

Educator collaboration is no longer an option for school librarians. Long gone are the days when practitioners could feel satisfaction delivering a quality program isolated from the general curriculum and the classroom teachers who implement it. Students are served best when educators collaboratively plan and coordinate their instruction. Collaboration basics are covered later in this book in Chapter Ten. The following approaches that enhance collaborative units include essential questions, problem-based learning, cooperative learning, teaching toward literacies, and using graphic organizers. They present opportunities for rich discussion and fresh learning experiences for the lucky students who will benefit from these best practices.

ESSENTIAL QUESTIONS

Research current curriculum design models and you will find that the essential question plays a major role in determining instructional decisions. Understanding by Design, the backward design curriculum model developed by Grant Wiggins and Jay McTighe in the late 1990s (2004) uses the term "big idea." Instruction is designed backward from identifying the desired learning outcomes, determining acceptable evidence of learning, and then designing appropriate learning experiences. Questions are along the lines of "Why study the topic?", "What makes the study of the topic universal?", "What is the Big Idea or the larger concept?", and "What is the value of such a study?" The simple distinction between "What are we learning today?" and "Why are we learning this today?" clarifies the difference that exists between essential questions and traditional instructional design that is derived from a topic of study and not from an inquiry approach to that study.

> To be able to be caught up into the world of thought—that is being educated.
> Edith Hamilton, American educator and author, 1867–1963

Essential questions serve as natural discussion prompts. Discussions tend to find students relating to the topic with prior knowledge and experiences. Strategies such as **Question the Author (QtA)** transform students into critical thinkers as they ask, "Who wrote this? What point was the author trying to make? What else could have been said? Whose voice is missing?" (Ogle, Klemp, and McBride 2008, 19).

Essential questions must be grounded in real-world accountability to be eligible for consideration by educators as they reflect and plan instruction. Surprisingly, standards serve to make that connection between essential questions and units of study. Learning standards have that unfortunate connotation with national and state standardized assessments. Looking at learning standards with fresh eyes allows us to view them as big ideas that are indeed worthwhile learning. The progression then leads to framing essential questions to guide our learning. How do we take that next step? We take the standard and rephrase it into a question that captures the essence of the issue at hand. If every standard were rephrased into an essential question, inquiry would become the center of learning and students would have greater ownership over their own learning processes.

> We learn more by looking for the answer to a question and not finding it than we do from learning the answer itself.
> Lloyd Alexander, American author, 1924–2007

PROBLEM-BASED LEARNING

Problem-based learning is an educational method that engages both self-directed and team research skills. Typically, an **authentic**, or real-world, problem is posed. Students first must activate prior knowledge, determine a research strategy, and develop viable solutions to messy, ill-defined situational problems or tales. The pattern of problem-based learning is an increasingly more self-directed learning process, with team members working both individually and together to solve problems. Problem-based learning becomes authentic in the real-world problem, application, and collaboration with community and global resources.

The use of **Conditional Instruction** where conditional terms such as *could be, might be, another way to think about it, one idea, no one knows for sure, usually but not always, a different approach* engages students in learning as actively participating in the determination of the authority of the information and is a worthy strategy to be coupled with problem-based learning (Ritchhart 1998, 140–141). In *College Knowledge: What It Really Takes for Students to Succeed and What We Can Do to Get Them Ready,* David T. Conley (2008) posits that college students who come from high schools that effectively prepared them understand that knowledge is **Discipline-Specific**; that there are theories and principles that guide learning in the disciplines; and that acquisition of knowledge in the disciplines is distinct and requires specific skills and habits of mind.

> It won't do you a bit of good to know everything if you don't do anything with it.
> Louise Fitzhugh, *Harriet the Spy,* 1964

COOPERATIVE LEARNING

Cooperative learning is a popular teaching strategy based on social learning theory. Typically, students of different ability groups are placed in the same group with specific tasks to perform. The effectiveness of **Differentiated Instruction,** which is a proactive teaching strategy based on the reality that one size does not fit all, depends on educators knowing their students and planning for readiness, interest, and ability differences. Teachers and school librarians who collaboratively and strategically plan for cooperative groups and tasks implement differentiated instruction with heightened knowledge of their students from multiple perspectives; students benefit from educators who know them in a variety of ways and apply that knowledge to planning for instruction.

Along with students enjoying the cooperative learning experiences, research indicates that social skills and improved attitude toward school are outcomes of this strategy. The **Jigsaw** method is one way to build these skills—by having students working in groups (sometimes called pods) that are responsible for collecting information on a given topic and then sharing this with other groups.

✓ Groups research and investigate assigned topics from a list determined by class discussion. Library tables work well as "Jigsaw Stations" to place a variety of materials on assigned topic.

✓ Each group member migrates to another group and is responsible for teaching these students about their topic.

✓ Members of each group return to their original group to have a follow-up discussion, bringing back content from the "Jigsaw" experience. A group discussion follows after all topics are taught.

TEACHING TOWARD LITERACIES

So many literacies, so little time. Information literacy reigns supreme with school librarians, but media, visual, and digital literacies are all vying for second place and have so many overlapping principles that it is becoming increasingly difficult to embed one without the others in collaboratively planned units. Digital literacy might engage the learner in actuating the resource, visual literacy in comprehending meaning from an image, and media literacy from the source and therefore bias of the producer of the image. And, finally, we might evaluate the information found in the image or text for authority, validity, credibility, and relevance to the information need at hand.

> Think left and think right
> and think low and think high,
> Oh, the THINKS you can think up
> if only you try!
> Dr. Seuss, *Oh, The THINKS You Can Think!*, 1975

GRAPHIC ORGANIZERS

From Donna Ogle's famous K-W-L charts to concept maps and webs, these instructional tools support students by visually and explicitly representing the learning and thinking process. They deserve their own category in this list of strategies because graphic organizers seem to invite multiple perspectives and representations of learning, which is a perfect fit for our learning environment. The one caveat is when the graphic organizer itself is presumed to be the learning goal—it is best applied as a tool to further thinking through the learning process, but not as an end in and of itself.

> It is important that students bring a certain ragamuffin, barefoot irreverence to their studies; they are not here to worship what is known, but to question it.
> Jacob Bronowski, British mathematician and biologist, 1908–1974

School librarians teach individual, small groups, and whole classes of students, teachers, administrators, parents, community members, and each other. In each instance a variety of instructional strategies might be called into action. The nimble grace of "natural teachers" is what we might consider to be the art of our craft. We recognize those among us who have seemingly endless patience with learners and relish in the challenge of unlocking the right instructional strategy for the right learner at the right time.

As learners ourselves, we each have a unique learning style, and it is only natural to have a tendency to utilize instructional strategies that match those ways in which we choose to learn. Take stock, look around, spread your wings, and reach for strategies that might stretch your comfort zone. We have a responsibility to all learners and therefore to teach in a variety of methods using numerous strategies. Learn from teachers who challenge your status quo, continue to be open to instructional strategies, and invite collaborative planning opportunities that might be realized in both the library and the classroom. Find and follow your teaching passion in brain research, emotional intelligence, gaming, or synectics. As a teacher in a learning environment that encompasses the world's knowledge, there are no limits to the connections and development that we could foster in all our students.

REFERENCES

Conley, D. T. 2008. *College knowledge: What it really takes for students to succeed and what we can do to get them ready.* New York: John Wiley.

Dewey, J. 1902/1990. *The child and the curriculum.* Chicago: University of Chicago.

Ogle, D., R. Klemp, and B. McBride. 2007. *Building literacy in social studies: Strategies for improving comprehension and critical thinking.* Alexandria, VA: Association for Supervision and Curriculum Development.

Ritchhart, R. 2002. *Intellectual character: What it is, why it matters, and how to get it.* San Francisco: Jossey-Bass.

Wiggins, G., and J. McTighe. 2004. *Understanding by design.* Alexandria, VA: Association for Supervision and Curriculum Development.

QUESTIONS AND ANSWERS ABOUT INSTRUCTIONAL STRATEGIES

1. Yes, I *am* a teacher among my other school librarian roles and I am comfortable teaching in the library. But here is my question. My teachers are so focused on the content and the skills that *they* are teaching that I am afraid that if I interject some other strategies that they might not be familiar with and that do not serve their direct curricular need that they will feel like I am off-task and confusing their students. Am I just being paranoid thinking that this could all backfire on me?

    We could not have stated a rationale for collaboratively planning library lessons any better. Connecting instructional strategies to the teacher's identified learning outcomes for a lesson plan or unit of study is your starting place. The discussion of what you propose to do empowers the teacher by broadening his or her perspective on ways to teach process skills. The more instructional strategies you have in your repertoire, the better. This will happen over time with experience. Flexibility in serving all students needs is a strength we can promote through those instructional strategies that highlight multiple perspectives on topics and range from lower- to higher-order thinking skills. Teach and learn along with your educators as you plan for instruction in both the classroom and the library; ask questions about the classroom implementation of the lesson so that you will consider best practices most appropriate to the teacher's style and focus.

2. I have a confession to make. I left the classroom after one year because teaching was just not my strength. I love that I have multiple roles in the school library, and I am passionate about issues such as intellectual freedom and advocacy, but I think that my teachers (I was in the same building as a classroom teacher) are well aware of my weaknesses. I was somewhat comforted when I learned that in some states the school librarians were not classroom teachers previously. They must be novices too. So it seems almost hypocritical of me to expect teachers to share their teaching with me through collaborative planning. Maybe the students are better off with my library being separate, just for selecting books and finding online resources for research projects.

So you were a classroom teacher for one year in one grade level. Now you have an opportunity to share your passion through instructional strategies at many grade levels. If you taught second grade, maybe the older students are a better fit for you; if you taught older students, you have a new opportunity to share your passion with the little ones. Don't think of instructional strategies solely as delivering the content of the general curriculum, but consider how you could advocate for intellectual freedom within particular units. Embed your passion, understand that you will make a lasting impression on students that you might not have taught otherwise, and accept this challenge to explore, discover, and learn to implement instructional strategies as a partner to your teachers.

READ MORE ABOUT INSTRUCTIONAL STRATEGIES

Dewey, J. 1938. *Experience and education*. Chicago: University of Chicago.

It is hard to select just one title but in this book Dewey most emphatically discusses what we would call authentic or real-world learning and dismisses all else as imposters posing as education. Worth rereading if it has been awhile.

Donham, J. 2008. *Enhancing teaching and learning: A leadership guide for school library media specialists* (2nd ed.). NY: Neal-Schuman.

Hands down, the best of the texts that connects school libraries directly to the curriculum. Both comprehensive and accessible, Donham has updated her second edition with the 2007 AASL Standards for 21st-Century Learners.

Jossey-Bass reader on teaching. 2003. San Francisco: Jossey-Bass.

Readings include articles and book excerpts written by William Ayers, Paulo Friere, Maxine Greene, Vivian Gussin Paley, Herbert Kohl, Lisa Delpit, Seymour Sarason, Martin Haberman, Frank Smith, and others. It is the passion of teaching that takes center stage; this volume is a one-stop shop for understanding the heart of teaching.

Marzano, R. J. 2007. *The art and science of teaching: A comprehensive framework for effective instruction*. Alexandria, VA: Association for Supervision and Curriculum Development.

Each chapter answers a question, such as "What will I do to establish and communicate learning goals, track student progress, and celebrate success?" The chapters include a classroom tale, research and theory, and realistic action steps.

Marzano, R. J., D. J. Pickering, and J. E. Pollock. 2001. *Classroom instruction that works: Research-based strategies for increasing student achievement*. Alexandria, VA: Association for Supervision and Curriculum Development.

Nine research-based strategies are explored, including summarizing and note taking; cooperative learning; and cues, questions, and advance organizers. Many strategies could easily be incorporated into library lessons; for example, a question such as "What if Cinderella had run into a major thunderstorm and never made it to the ball?" might be posed by a literary meteorologist.

Ogle, D., R. Klemp, and B. McBride. 2007. *Building literacy in social studies: Strategies for improving comprehension and critical thinking*. Alexandria, VA: Association for Supervision and Curriculum Development.

Literacies specific to social studies discussed include teaching strategies for textbook literacy; interpreting primary and secondary documents; evaluating Internet sources; and specific strategies for newspaper and magazine literacy. Research-based strategies focus on fostering engaged learning, vocabulary development for older students, and on civic engagement. Visual literacy teaching methods use maps, photographs, images, political cartoons, charts, and graphs.

CONNECT INSTRUCTIONAL STRATEGIES TO 21ST-CENTURY LEARNERS

School librarians strive to match the right instructional strategy to the right student at the right time. We model matching strategies to information needs and the flexibility to adjust those strategies as the learning process progresses. We model these intellectual behaviors over time and over many content areas as only we can, through the school library media program serving our students for their entire tenures in our schools. Our students who excel demonstrate adaptability by changing the inquiry focus, questions, resources, or strategies when necessary to achieve success (1.2.5).

Our best practices in instructional strategies encourage students to use both divergent and convergent thinking to formulate alternative conclusions and test them against the evidence (2.2.2). The recursive information process comes into action as students test conclusions and develop new information tasks. School librarians who are particularly comfortable leading discussions, asking probing questions, and modeling thinking-aloud strategies model higher-level thinking skills that are easily transferable to the classroom. These types of explorations beg for the variety of alternative reading materials accessible in exemplary school libraries.

The Dispositions in Action in our third standard, "Share knowledge and participate ethically and productively as members of our democratic society," are all encompassed within cooperative learning teaching methods (3.2.1; 3.2.2; 3.2.3). Modeling the demonstration of leadership and confidence within the team and showing social responsibility situates the school librarian as having an additional role within the teaching role, that of the guide in the zone of proximal development. Learning alongside our students while guiding their discovery is a subtle yet powerful instructional strategy that exemplifies the art of the teaching role of the school librarian.

DISPOSITIONAL QUESTIONS ABOUT INSTRUCTIONAL STRATEGIES

1. The social learning environment of the school library sounds lovely in the abstract, but the students in our middle school simply need more structure. Their classroom instruction is so tailored that anything that smacks of multiple perspectives, conditional instruction, cooperative learning, or problem-based learning sends them into orbit. Then "classroom management" becomes an issue, and the library is a miserable place for everyone. When students have not experienced collaboratively planned library lessons in their elementary schools and their middle school classroom instruction is just about scripted, how do we expect even the best of the best practices in instructional strategies to have an impact? Where do I go from here?

2. I believe that our special education students can learn to research and our bilingual students can learn through visual literacy. Who am I to take on all the "powers that be" who think that the purpose of the school library is to support the grade-level curriculum and to implement the packaged reading programs for our independent reading function? Now, everything that I stated that I believe means extra work for me, but I think that it is all in a day's work in serving all students in a quality school library media program. However, even I don't know where I got these ideas; I did not learn about serving our special education or English language learners when I was in library school. I learned about rubrics, graphic organizers, and cooperative learning, as if all students are the same in every class. I collaboratively plan with classroom teachers; I implement best practices instructional strategies; I am ready to take the next step, but I am not finding support in our field. Am I out of step? Any ideas for me?

> ## *Chapter Three*

Information Literacy

It used to be that students learned everything they needed from textbooks, and teachers were the prime dispensers of knowledge, but these days are long gone. At one time, information was published mostly in print format by mainstream publishers, who fact-checked information to ensure accuracy, but today anyone can publish his or her thoughts on a Web site, blog, Wiki, Flickr, or in Wikipedia. Aspiring authors are able to bypass traditional publishers altogether to self-publish and market their own books, which can be economical and timely but puts the onus on the reader to determine credibility. There is a name for this condition in which so much information is being produced in so many different formats that it is difficult to assimilate or absorb. It is *information overload*. In these days of informational quicksand, what is one to do?

LISA

Really? Another set of national standards? New benchmarks? It is hard not just to think, "OK, whatever," even though it makes sense that we have to keep changing the standards with the times. I just feel as though I was tricked. I spent my last two years working on library skills and placing them at different places in the curriculum—and now this change. And the district is considering what to do about technology standards and how the library program might be involved with that new-joy-I-mean-project.

My teachers are friendly enough, but we are just all doing our own thing. If I want to teach library skills and call them information literacy skills, that is fine with them. They are happy that I pay attention to what they are teaching and do what I can to adapt what I do in the library to their curriculum. I am starting to feel more confident that the way I teach library skills fits into the George Washington Elementary School (WES) the way that it should. My principal, Dr. Kelly, has high standards for excellence overall but does not say anything about the Learning Resource Center (LRC) one way or the other. It feels like no news is good news.

So I do things such as have the fourth graders stand at the shelves where their books will be shelved when they write them. At first, I have them pick a card from a bucket—they might have written a novel or a biography or a book about tsunamis. One half of the class stands at the shelves and the other half has to check that they are at the correct spot. Reverse, repeat, and eventually everyone stands at their shelves. The next time they are in the LRC, I let them choose what they might write about and stand at the appropriate range. We go through the LRC with everyone explaining why they are standing where they are. I created that lesson, although I am sure other librarians do it too. The joke on me is that I know that at the high school the librarians pull the books and the students do not need to know how their LRC is organized. So now I will look for what I am already doing in the standards for 21st-century learners and fix my old lessons with new numbers. Again, no doubt what everyone else is doing.

LET'S DISCUSS INFORMATION LITERACY

It is precisely the challenge of *information overload* that has breathed new life into the role of the school librarian. No other educator in the school is better suited to teach students the skills to manage, evaluate, analyze, and synthesize large amounts of information than the school librarian. What we bring to the party is our ability to model the disposition of information literacy for students to become *discerning* and critical thinkers who can apply, analyze, synthesize, and evaluate information through a process of analysis, inference, explanation, interpretation, evaluation, and self-regulation (Taylor 2005, 112–113).

> We drive into the future using only our rear view mirror.
>
> Marshall McLuhan, Canadian educator, philosopher, and scholar, 1911–1980

The notion of information literacy has gone mainstream. Thomas L. Friedman (2005), author of *The World Is Flat: A Brief History of the Twenty-First Century,* suggests that globalization, fueled by personal computers and fiber optics, has leveled playing fields between industrial and emerging countries. In a flat world, marked by uncertainty and change, jobs flow between borders depending on the skill set of workers and the need for products and services. Ways of doing and thinking can change in an instant, as new information, knowledge, and conditions present themselves. People, as well as organizations, who cannot recognize and respond quickly to changing events, information, and perspectives will likely face obsolescence. To fight obsolescence, people must commit to lifelong learning, sharpen and keep skill sets up-to-date, and develop collaborative abilities to work with colleagues who represent various ethnicities and perspectives, no matter where they work—down the hall or halfway around the world. Underlying global competitiveness is the need for students to become creative and critical thinkers who can connect the dots between seemingly unrelated events to recognize emerging patterns. In this environment in which we live, knowing facts is not as important as being *discerning.* School librarians help students become discerning by teaching information literacy.

In the late 1980s, *Information Power: Guidelines for School Library Media Programs* changed the mission of school library programs from "teaching facts in a book in the library's collection" to making students and staff effective users of ideas and

> People believe almost anything they see in print.
>
> E. B. White, *Charlotte's Web,* 1952

information through *systematic* learning activities that develop cognitive strategies for selecting, retrieving, analyzing, evaluating, synthesizing, and creating information (Taylor 2005, 14). *Information Power* moved us away from teaching how to access and find resources and toward knowing what to do with the information once it is found. A complementary piece to the puzzle is the American Association of School Librarian's *Standards for the 21st-Century Learner,* which was unveiled at its October 2007 conference in Reno, Nevada. School librarians are responsible for ensuring that students can meet the four standards as well as the strands—the skills, dispositions in action, responsibilities, and self-assessment strategies of the information literate.

> Everyone gets so much information all day long that they lose their common sense.
>
> Gertrude Stein, American writer, 1874–1946

The first step towards implementing a schoolwide information literacy approach is to be information literate *yourself.* Learn all you can about information literacy by attending workshops, reading, and studying and developing a professional develop-

ment plan to grow in this area. You are the model of information literacy. You cannot teach information literacy unless *you* are information literate and using information to inform personal and professional decisions.

When we teach information literacy "what is being taught is a research process" (Taylor 2005, 84). Although there are several research models, such as the Big6™, FLIP IT!™, the Information Search Process, Pathways to Knowledge®, and the Research Process, each helps students understand the basic steps in the research process, which are to identify a problem, find information, synthesize the gathered information into a product or project, and evaluate the product or project (Taylor 2005, 84).

The second step is to construct an inquiry-based learning environment in which students are invited to grapple with complicated and "messy" issues and questions by recognizing the interrelatedness of the world and how it is becoming more so. The foundation for this step is to create collaborative instructional opportunities that require students to consider complex situations in which no one answer suffices. School librarians do this by developing a collection that supports thoughtful debate and dialog and gently pushes students beyond their comfort zones and perspectives. School librarians understand that continuing to adhere to and pro-

mote a "black and white" perspective does little to position students to succeed in a world experiencing accelerated change and runs counter to the AASL *Standards for the 21st-Century Learner* supporting an inquiry-based approach (1.1.1), flexibility (2.2.1), a critical stance (2.2.3), and diverse and global perspectives (2.3.2).

> You are educated. Your certification is in your degree. You may think of it as the ticket to the good life. Let me ask you to think of an alternative. Think of it as your ticket to change the world.
>
> Tom Brokaw, American journalist

Your role in helping students become information literate stems from good instructional practice. It is not uncommon in schools to see "bird units," which David Loertscher (n.d.), author and professor of library science at San Jose State University in California, describes as "low-level cut and paste activities, such as transferring facts from library resources on to worksheets or just cutting information off the Internet to paste in a report." Little comes out of these bird unit-type explorer, state, or "old famous dead men" projects except plagiarism (ibid). Each bird unit that is taught is a lost opportunity to develop and nurture the creative thinking that is needed to thrive in a world in flux. Boring lessons requiring little thought hamper the student's ability to compete in a global and competitive economy suited for creative, multidimensional, and culturally competent world citizens.

> **Information is not knowledge.**
> Albert Einstein, German theoretical physicist
> and winner of the 1921 Nobel Prize in Physics,
> 1879–1955

Students know when they are being cheated by classroom teachers and school librarians who design bird units requiring little effort to complete, and they yearn for engaging classes. Cushman (2006), who interviewed 65 students to gather their perspectives on high school culture and climate, writes that when "classes offer only a steady diet of tedium, these students would just as soon forget about school and look to the media, the streets, or peer relationships for interest and stimulation" (34).

The culminating step is to take information literacy schoolwide by implementing a formal program that Joie Taylor (2006) describes in *Information Literacy and the School Library Media Center*, which is an invaluable resource for doing this. Implementing an information literacy program requires school librarians to rely on their dispositions of leadership (Chapter Twelve), advocacy (Chapter Nine), and communication (Chapter Eight) to persuade teachers and administrators that critical thinking, a by-product of engaging learning opportunities, is likely when everyone—school librarians included—work together to make learning the engaging process it is meant to be.

> For having lived long, I have experienced many instances of being obliged, by better information or fuller consideration, to change opinions, even on important subjects, which I once thought right but found to be otherwise.
> Benjamin Franklin, American diplomat,
> scientist, inventor, and Founding Father,
> 1706–1790

REFERENCES

American Association of School Librarians, and Association for Educational Communications and Technology. 1998. *Information power: Building partnerships for learning.* Chicago: American Library Association.

Cushman, K. 2006. Help us care enough to learn. *Educational Leadership* 63(5): 34–37.

Friedman, T. L. 2005. *The world is flat: A brief history of the twenty-first century.* New York: Farrar, Straus, and Giroux.

Loertscher, D. n.d. *Ban those bird units model testing an action research project.* Retrieved March 20, 2009 from http://www.txla.org/conference/SLS/Ban%20Those%20Birds.pdf

Taylor, J. 2006. *Information literacy and the school library media center.* Westport, CT: Libraries Unlimited.

QUESTIONS AND ANSWERS ABOUT INFORMATION LITERACY

1. What is the difference between information literacy and a research model?

    In my district, we are all expected to teach one particular model and use it with all our classes. I am told that this is information literacy, but it sounds to me like there is more to this. Some school librarians apply a research model to what seems to me to be a "bird unit" and think they are helping students become critical thinkers. Is this all there is to information literacy?

    The nuts and bolts of information literacy is a research model, but the foundation of information literacy is engaging lessons based on sound instructional strategies. Applying the research process to a passive lesson does little but require students to learn one more thing unconnected to their life. The first step is to collaborate to create dynamic learning opportunities. Understanding the reason for promoting information literacy is important too, because we want to encourage students to think creatively, take intellectual chances, and have fun learning. The basic information literacy research model has five steps: defining the research problem, finding information, extracting information, developing a product or project, and evaluation; these steps provide us with a sequence of information use and "ensure consistent development of needed skills and strategies so students can retrieve, access, process, and share information" (Taylor 2006, 83). However, as you collaborate with teachers to develop information literacy opportunities within a lesson, you want to ensure that the process is rigorous and meaningful. You will need to model each step of the research process, but especially the analysis and synthesis of information.

2. I understand how important information literacy is, and it bothers me that so many students in this school do cute "techie" projects that to me do not seem very meaningful. I try to encourage a bit more rigor, but nobody wants to hear this message. On top of that, I seem to have everything going against me. The school does not have a culture of collaboration, and the library's fixed schedule ensures that I will not be collaborating anytime soon. Whenever I start to say something about information literacy, eyes start rolling and I can almost hear teachers saying, "Please spare me . . . I don't need another thing to do." I want to do more than check out books, read stories, and teach students to use the encyclopedia. Each month when I make a student loan payment, I wonder why I went to graduate school for this. How can I begin doing some information literacy activities even in my situation?

    To become the information hub on the school requires leadership, advocacy, and collaboration. You can think of school libraries a little like Newton's First Law of Motion (the one about inertia). A mass will keep doing what it is doing unless something acts upon it. If the library is limping along, it will take considerable effort to create an instructionally sound, collaborative, heart-of-the-school type of library. You will have to speak out. Read the chapter on leadership. Leadership is influence. Identify your message about information literacy, and reiterate to teachers that this is not another thing to add to their already overfull plates, but a change in focus that will actually make their jobs easier as students' cognitive skills increase and they become independent thinkers less likely to want spoon-feeding. Then reread Chapter Ten on Collaboration. Identify one or two teachers who are open to new ideas and willing to collaborate with you; begin to apply a research model to their curriculum. In a flat world, the best gift we give to our students is information literacy.

READ MORE ABOUT INFORMATION LITERACY

Kuhlthau, C. C., L. K Maniotes, and A. K. Caspari. 2007. *Guided inquiry: Learning in the 21st-century school*. Westport, CT: Libraries Unlimited.

Kuhlthau, Maniotes, and Caspari provide the foundation to understand and use the process of guided inquiry—as preparation for lifelong learning—to meet the informational and educational needs of 21st-century learners.

Lorenzen, M. 2005. *LibraryInstruction.com: The librarian's weapon of mass instruction*. http://www.libraryinstruction.com.

This site contains articles to understand information literacy, as well as lesson plans. This site received recognition by the JoeAnt Site of the Month in September 2003. JoeAnt recognizes interesting and worthy-of-a-visit sites.

Taylor, J. 2006. *Information literacy and the school library media center*. Westport, CT: Libraries Unlimited.

Taylor's book is an overview of the information literacy process and its implementation throughout all curricula areas, as well as the importance of collaboration, leadership, and instruction and learning. The author discusses all commonly known information processing models and how information literacy skills are important in assisting students to meet state and national curriculum standards.

CONNECT INFORMATION LITERACY TO 21ST-CENTURY LEARNERS

In a flat world that is changing rapidly, students cannot be taught all they need to learn, because we ourselves are unsure what that entails. The best gift we can give to students is a learning environment that builds respect for lifelong learning, inquiry, and flexibility. The AASL *Standards for the 21st-Century Learner* inform our practice by helping us understand the range of dispositions of information literate students. The Standards articulate the behaviors that information literate students need in a dynamic and changing world—initiative, confidence, curiosity, adaptability, flexibility, leadership, teamwork, motivation, adaptability, a critical stance, divergent and convergent thinking, social responsibility, motivation, and an openness to new ideas.

School librarians who keep these dispositions in mind as they collaborate with teachers will likely create engaging and exciting lessons. In the United States, we have a large number of school dropouts, which could also be called a "disengagement" problem. If we had held a students' interests in the first place with compelling and challenging lessons, we would not be facing a 30 to 40 percent dropout rate.

An example is Disposition in Action 1.2.1—to "display initiative and engagement by posing questions and investigating the answers beyond the collection of superficial facts"—which provides school librarians the opportunity to develop lessons that challenge students. Questioning is an important skill to teach because this frames what students are to learn, think, and consider, but it does not come naturally. By modeling the development of challenging questions, we are able to help students think more deeply.

DISPOSITIONAL QUESTIONS ABOUT INFORMATION LITERACY

1. I am concerned about plagiarism because we do a lot of "bird units" at my school. Everybody seems to do it and they don't seem to care that it is wrong. Each year I have been at this school, I see the same thing—one teacher in particular brings students to the library to search for information on the Internet. He instructs students to copy and paste the relevant passages into a blank document without much regard for citing the sources. I am appalled by this type of research and offered to help, but he tells me he doing just fine by himself. He says that his students are just fine researching this way—after all, he says, ""Databases are becoming obsolete and if you cannot find it on Google, then it is not worth knowing." There is so much to address—plagiarism, instructional strategy, information literacy, and collaboration. Where do I even begin?

2. There is a shortage of school librarians in my district. Last year I was working at the public library, and now I find myself "teaching" at a school that supports information literacy. I am not sure teaching is the right word to use, because I know nothing about what students are supposed to learn and less about teaching them information literacy skills. At the public library, we pretty much answered reference questions for patrons and did all their researching for them. I am pretty good at collection development and reference, but a large class of students is very intimidating to me. Some teachers are more understanding than others and try to help me with the lesson, but I am wishing I had never decided to leave my old job. I am stuck and need to learn how to teach. My principal has heard through the grape-vine that there is problem and wants to meet with me next week. She says I need to come to this meeting with a professional development plan to improve my teaching of informations literacy. I am so lost. I do not know where to begin. Can you help?

Chapter Four

Assessment

There are educators who think about assessment in the broad terms of high-stakes national standardized exams and those who feel more personally affronted by the time-consuming tasks of grading written compositions and research reports. Are you one of the many who were motivated to take the plunge into the school library because there was no grading? Or at the very least, was that one benefit of the learning environment as you considered the profession? If not, surely you know others who feel that, if we must assess, nothing is sacred and the thrill is gone. Perhaps an exploration of assessment and how this term is defined within the context of the school library will influence your thinking, calm your nerves, and inform your practice.

DONNA

Unless you have taught high school English as a full-time teacher, you do not understand what it means to give students "feedback." Try grading 150 themes, over and over again, by hand—now some teachers are grading online. Okay, that is the extreme. Don't think that it was not attractive moving into the library where there is no grading. But have a conversation with a teacher who says that in his discipline of math, or even use reading, that only scientifically researched best practices are used. Sean's question to me is this: How do I know that the way I am teaching his students how to do research is the best way to do it. I look at him and I think about three things: (1) I don't know; (2) I am so happy that it does not matter; (3) I wonder how Sean and his wife are doing with the new baby—he looks tired and now they have two kids under the age of three. No one has ever asked me about any kind of evaluation or grading or assessment in the Abraham Lincoln High School

(LHS) library. And finally, here is an appropriate time to "shhhh" somebody. Maybe the question will go away. Or not.

I started asking around just to see what other high school librarians are doing, and it seems that some of them use a number of online measures to test research skills. They must have support staff all day long. My strategy remains keeping my head down on this one. No one is mentioning it in our district or in the feeder schools. I just see it as a can of worms. Nothing we do in the library is officially assessed. So to get back to answering Sean's question, I answer by talking about the independent learning that goes on in the library and how assessment would actually be an unwelcome barrier to learning for our students, and I hope that will hold, for a while at least. And I have to say, with all due respect, I would love to throw him into the world of English teacher assessments for just one grading quarter. I think it would be a real eye-opener for anyone.

LET'S DISCUSS ASSESSMENT

In 1949, University of Chicago education scholar Ralph W. Tyler published a series of lectures in a small but powerful book entitled *Basic Principles of Curriculum and Instruction.* In this seminal text, Tyler posited four basic questions before educators: (1) What is worthwhile to learn? (2) How should it be taught? (3) When should it be taught? (4) How do we evaluate learning? Tyler set education on a path of writing curriculum in the form of student behavioral learning objectives, and his graduate students, Benjamin Bloom, Hilda Taba, and others who followed, were instrumental in defining elements of curriculum based on Tyler's four questions.

> We don't know a millionth of one percent about anything.
> Thomas Alva Edison, American inventor, 1847–1931

Many curriculum models later, Grant Wiggins and Jay McTighe (1998, 2005) provide a backward design for curriculum design that follows Tyler's most essential of questions: What is worthwhile learning? Wiggins and McTighe begin with the outcomes of learning, and, with that fundamental step, they transport assessment from only one traditional understanding of the term to a more purposeful place in the process of learning. Our exploration will distinguish assessment in a few ways, beginning with the concept of educative or formative assessment and summative or evaluative assessment; types of formative and summative assessments; and tools of assessment. Assessment for advocacy defines the role of assessment as evidence of our vital teaching role through the school library program. And finally, self-assessment strategies will be discussed in the section called Connect Assessment to 21st-Century Learners.

EDUCATIVE OR FORMATIVE ASSESSMENT is assessment for learning. It is the ongoing process of adjusting and readjusting that occurs over the course of learning new content, integrating it with prior knowledge, building new connections and patterns, and using the knowledge in a new way to build understanding. Much of this process is internalized by the learner and intuited by the astute educator, who acts in the role of a guide or facilitator of learning. Educative assessment is designed to teach the learner what is worthwhile learning—as the learning is ongoing through meaningful feedback that is timely and purposeful (Wiggins 1998, 12). In receiving this data from the teacher, the student focuses on the valuable lessons within a unit of study. Consider the performance tasks of playing a sport or having a role in a performing arts production. The role of the teacher is akin to that of the coach, who guides learning through practices, with each practice getting closer to reaching the goal of a performance. The performance itself becomes a learning opportunity to achieve higher goals.

Types of formative assessment include observation, portfolio, authentic, journaling, workshops, conferences, and use of exemplars. Observation is a natural skill for an effective teacher and has an impact on the efficacy of the following types of ongoing assessment: portfolio assessments require that students collect and reflect upon artifacts (formative assessments may be included) produced in the process of the unit of study; authentic assessments are student-centered, real-world applications of understanding that might either mimic the actual event or engage students in community demonstrations of learning; journaling, or logging, requires that students keep a running account of learning experiences and usually requires reflection and planning; workshops and conferences require students to meet with teachers in small groups or individually to discuss ongoing research, review first drafts, and determine progress and next steps; and the use of prior student work as exemplars demonstrates what constitutes proficiency in the learning experience.

SUMMATIVE OR EVALUATIVE ASSESSMENT is the assessment *of* learning. This assessment is the traditional audit of the performance, resulting in a grade at the conclusion of a unit of study. This assessment is developed as a fixed standard, predetermined based on curriculum goals within the content area and grade level. Summative assessment is usually considered to be a single measure of achievement. Although the teacher is ultimately responsible for this assessment, there are various other methods of assessment that may be considered, even for the purposes of evaluation.

Types of summative assessment include the more formal and traditional quizzes, exams, rubrics, seatwork (or homework), final copies, and competitions. The national, regional, state, and district assessments are norm-referenced summative assessments. At the classroom, or "local" level of instruction, teachers are responsible for summative assessments but often are not instructed in the creation of assessments. Sometimes we all assume that our colleagues have professional education or training in practical applications, when, in fact, they are expected to create valid and reliable local assessments with little or no guidance. Some teachers also incorporate more creative demonstrations of learning, such as mock performances and authentic assessments, in addition to traditional unit exams or research projects.

Essential to the quality of each form of assessment is the validity, reliability, fairness, rigor, and usefulness (Wiggins 1998, 337). Our goal is to guide our learners with equity and meaning. Assessments that are valid measure what they are intended to measure and in the same manner that the content has been delivered; assessments that are reliable are independent of the person who is the assessor or of the time when the assessment is conducted; assessments that are fair are bias-free and are

> The best way to get a sure thing on a fact is to go and examine it for yourself, and not take anybody's say-so.
> Mark Twain, American author, 1835–1910

equitable to all students; assessments that have rigor have expectations that respect the student as a learner capable of achieving an appropriate level of understanding; assessments are useful

> Smooth seas do not make skillful sailors.
> African proverb

if they are contextually relevant and further the understanding of the learner.

TOOLS OF ASSESSMENT include instructional strategies and tools that are particularly purposeful for ongoing assessment, but they may also be used in combination in a portfolio format. Graphic organizers, checklists, rubrics, and research journals, or logs, are the most commonly used tools. Students working with rubrics might have mini-checklists that fit each criterion and match the varying ability levels indicated by the rubric. One caveat is to try to avoid going overboard with rubrics, etc. As effective as they are individually, there is a numbing effect that would be hard to overcome. Continuing to seek out new tools for ongoing assessment might involve adaptations—for example, take a multiple choice question, remove the answers, and change it into an open-ended prompt. Particular tools are often selected in keeping with personal teaching styles; savvy students who "do school well" pick up on teachers' predilections for instruction. Virtual tools of assessment are readily available and are easily embedded in teacher Web sites.

ASSESSMENT FOR ADVOCACY AS EVIDENCE OF LEARNING includes making informed decisions about each of our students and acting as responsible educators. It requires us to focus on high-quality, relevant assessments in every learning environment in every learning engagement. Libraries are not immune if librarians want to be effective teachers along with being information professionals. Demystifying assessment from the dark cloud of national testing to the local brand of formative assessments allows us to reflect in new ways about this responsibility as educators. We serve our students better, and we advocate for our role in their academic achievement using evidence from lessons integrating the library into the curriculum across content areas. We must have a strong stance to present the evidence based on assessments and the ability to interpret the results. What appears to be a disaster might indicate a need for more current resources in a particular area of the library collection; or, perhaps, mutual planning time scheduled into the school day; or support staffing that allows for the librarian to co-teach instead of conducting clerical tasks. Initial ventures into assessment for advocacy and collecting evidence should be viewed as baseline data from which to build a better library program and not a personal commentary on the librarian. It's not about us; it is about best serving the students.

December 11, 1953
My Dear Prof. Einstein,
   Today in school my class reported on famous immigrants. One committee had to report on your life and why you are famous. We got into a discussion of your theory. We found out that your theory is about relativity, but we don't know what relativity is.
   I would appreciate it if you could send me some information best explaining relativity and what it is, and also some interesting facts about your life.
                              Thank you,
                              Richard, age 11
Alice Calaprice and Evelyn Einstein, *Dear Professor Einstein: Albert Einstein's Letters to and from Children*, 2002

REFERENCES

Callison, D. 1993. The potential for portfolio assessment. *School Library Media Annual* 11:30–39.

Kuhlthau, C. C. 1994. *Assessment and the school library media center.* Englewood, CO: Libraries Unlimited.

Neely, T. Y., and J. Ferguson. 2006. Developing information literacy assessment instruments. In *Information literacy assessment: Standards-based tools and assignments,* ed. by Teresa Y. Neely, 153–171. Chicago: American Library Association.

Stripling, B. K. 1993. Practicing authentic assessment in the school library. In *School Library Media Annual,* ed. Carol Kuhlthau, 40–57. Englewood, CO: Libraries Unlimited.

Wiggins, G. 1998. *Educative assessment: Designing assessments to inform and improve student performance.* San Francisco: Jossey-Bass.

QUESTIONS AND ANSWERS ABOUT ASSESSMENT

1. Here is another example of the field being out of touch with what is happening at the building level in the schools. All that my district members, and therefore my teachers, care about regarding the topic of assessment is the standardized tests. They do not talk about assessment except as a necessary evil. I feel that, if I start bringing it up, it will go over like a lead balloon. So my self-assessment would be to stay quiet.

    Without question, we need to go along to get along. However, as school librarians, we do listen to another drum beating as well. Teachers do not have to justify their existence, nor do they require the benevolence of an administration to have an impact on a budget, which, of course, by nature, has an impact on student learning, our eye on the prize. Our goal is to improve student learning. In order to do that, we need to provide evidence of student learning in connection with the library. The library requires funding for acquisition of current, relevant resources to support the curriculum. The assessments of learning in the library serve as assessments for advocacy because they are indicators of student learning. This way of thinking about our story becomes most powerful when student work is collected and used as evidence of learning; when pre- and post-benchmarks of learning information fluency are recorded; when students experience the learning that is inquiry-driven and do not want to stop the process. We have a story to tell, and we have a need to tell that story well. We hear different drums, we walk our path next to our teachers, but we do walk our own path. Be selective; start with one friendly teacher and talk about a formative assessment of one lesson. Chances are you are already doing it, but perhaps not collecting the data in an organized fashion. Think about it. How does that sound to you?

2. My school is exemplary; national tests are not an issue in our affluent demographic. Our students are above average (here in Lake Woebegone) and teachers think less of those who talk about assessment, as if they are not as dedicated to real learning as they

are. There actually is a lot of quality formative assessment going on, but I am just not a part of it in any sense of the word. So where does that leave me?

First of all, we are glad for the success of your students. But, even at the most affluent schools, there are students who have needs that could be met with more concerted efforts on their behalf. In your case, I might seek out those teachers who might feel that their students could use some extra attention, such as the special education, low-ability level, or English language learners. Oftentimes those teachers are very welcoming, approachable, and flexible. Another thought that bears attention is that we do not want to get caught up in terminology. Working with a teacher to initiate a peer critiquing activity during a research project is a wonderful example of formative assessment, but it does not need to carry that mantle. Collaborative planning using an outcomes-based curriculum design will get you where you want to go. Form follows function; work toward the best practice for your students, without regard for the official education jargon. Perhaps you ask a teacher to debrief after a unit of study is completed, and you model self-assessment strategies; follow-up by suggesting that next time, perhaps, the students could go through that process of reflection as an enhancement to the lesson. Each school is different, our teachers and students are different, and we all need to be responsive to our own learning communities.

READ MORE ABOUT ASSESSMENT

Farmer, L. S. J., and J. Henri. 2008. *Information literacy assessment in K–12 settings.* Lanham, MD: Scarecrow Press.

Farmer and Henri first share a historical perspective on information literacy and then emphasizes the critical nature of the school librarian's role in assessing for learning. Topics are broad-based and help the collaborative relationship with teacher colleagues. Specific steps for creating assessments include international examples.

Harada, V. H., and J. M. Yoshina. 2005. *Assessing learning: Librarians and teachers as partners.* Westport, CO: Libraries Unlimited.

Harada and Yoshina focus on the role of the school librarian in improving student learning. Assessment is an integral piece to that responsibility; the authors suggest how and what to assess. Written in an accessible manner, *Assessing Learning* provides specific tools appropriate for all grade levels. It is an excellent primer on the subject of assessing student learning as a critical element of the school librarian teaching role.

Harada, V. H., and J. M. Yoshina. 2006. Assessing learning: The missing piece in instruction? *School Library Media Activities Monthly. 22*(7): 20–23.

The situation often arises that different school librarians have concerns with their students' inability to retain information literacy taught in the LMC. Harada and Yoshina focus on a "shift from teaching focus to learning" and properly assess students' learning as a means of improving teaching in the LMC. Two illustrative examples with assessments are outlined; tips for new LMS; links to online tutorials; and a bibliography complete this substantive article.

Vance, A. L., and R. Nickel, eds. 2007. *Assessing student learning in the school library media center.* Chicago: American Association of School Librarians.

This AASL publication accompanies the fall forum on assessment of student learning that was held in Rhode Island in October 2006. Contributions by institute presenters include the following: Harada addresses the importance of assessing learning; Stripling presents an assessment of information fluency inquiry model; Dzikowski focuses on test question formulation; Pappas offers specific assessment tools; and Zmuda summarizes the forum by highlighting the partnership role in improvement planning.

Wiggins, G. 1998. *Educative assessment: Designing assessments to inform and improve student performance.* San Francisco: Jossey-Bass.

Wiggins's focus is on assessment *for* learning, using authentic tasks and providing ongoing feedback. Student understanding and learning are the focus rather than accountability, although grading and reporting are included in the text. This book helps the reader garner a solid understanding of performance-based evidence of learning.

CONNECT ASSESSMENT TO 21ST-CENTURY LEARNERS

The fourth category of each of the AASL 21st-Century Learner Standards is Self-Assessment Strategies. The reflection required to monitor our own learning processes effectively may be modeled by school librarians as they work with students individually, in groups, and in class discussions. Modeling thinking-aloud skills, dispositions, and responsibilities for each of the standards is a simple best practice to emulate. Reinforcing self-assessment behaviors by modeling them aloud allows students a glimpse of the process in action. This approach is in stark contrast to that of the educator who is uncomfortable learning in front of students. Transforming a question or topic into a research project focuses attention on the actual train of thought that eludes many students. Finding value in the dead ends of research and continuing to research down a different path or taking the recursive action of reformatting the research question are worthy demonstrations of inquiry learning. Inviting feedback from students, using it "to guide own inquiry process," and asking students for advice models standards 1.4.2 and 1.4.4. Following a path of determining whether to use students' advice; "reflecting on completeness of investigation; recognizing new knowledge and understanding; and developing directions for future investigations" encompasses all of the self-assessment strategies in Standard 2: learners use skills, resources, and tools to draw conclusions, make informed decisions, apply knowledge to new situations, and create new knowledge (2007).

Playing well with others and reflecting on the learning process indicate that "learners use skills, resources, and tools to share knowledge and participate ethically and productively as members of our democratic society," as stated in Standard 3. The self-assessment strategies identified in Standard 4, where students "pursue personal and aesthetic growth," have a human development connotation regarding one's consciousness and capacity growth and maturity. This is an area that might attract some teachers who are comfortable in the affective domain and have the reverse response from others who prefer the context of the content area. Standard 4 provides a foundation for library programming that appeals to students on a personal level at all ages and stages of development. "Identify own areas of interest" (4.4.1) is relevant to all learners and is a meaningful starting place for engaging young learners in the independent learning environment of the library.

DISPOSITIONAL QUESTIONS ABOUT ASSESSMENT

1. Our school is not performing well, and this might be the last year our principal is here. We think that she is doing a great job, and it will be terrible to lose her. Everyone is trying to keep her looking good for the parents and the community. Now is not the time to raise issues about assessment that are not already being discussed. I will be considered to be a troublemaker because of the school climate. Do I act upon embedding formative assessments in the library and maybe a few pre- and post-assessments quietly with a few close colleagues, or do I just not risk rocking the boat and my relationship with the teachers?

2. We have a teacher who is very traditional and very effective; she has high expectations of her students, and they try to match those expectations. She believes in the value of research but does not want me to help the students, to discuss the project with them as they are working on it, etc. This teacher thinks that some students will get preferential treatment and that will be unfair and inequitable. She conducts diagnostic assessments on her students, and she assigns them to different levels of projects based on those assessments. She represents the best and the worst all rolled into one pantsuit. Frankly, I am afraid to bring up assessment with her, because I know that I do not know enough to have an intelligent discussion; I don't think I could hold my own. However, I do believe that her class could provide great "evidence" of learning in the library—even if I cannot help the students. Oh, I am confused. Help.

The Right Book for the Right Child

Chapter Five

Literacy and Reading

Education scholar Frank Smith (1988) contends that "one of the most important communities any individual can join is the 'literacy club,' because membership ensures that individuals learn how to read and write, and because reading is the entrance to many other clubs" (vii). Children become "powerful literates" by participating in literate activities with people who know their way around the world of print (Meek 1991, 33). It is the habit of weaving literacy into one's life that we are inspired to model and infuse in our curriculum support and extracurricular programming. In guiding learners to reach their potential, we seek to support reading through the literacy environment of the school library and individually with our one-on-one interactions with students.

LISA

I am a science fiend and therefore, by nature, not a reader. Except that I do love to read about science in books, and some of the Web sites are so amazing now. I just never felt that that was what teachers meant by reading when I was in school. I want to change that. This sounds strange, but the way that I approach reading to my classes is to find the science in whatever we are reading. It makes it a challenge to me, so, if I think that it is fun, I will do a better job of sharing that attitude with my young scholars.

How do I do that? Take folktales for instance. For some reason, almost all the teachers at WES are crazy about folktales. I think that they are useful for lots of different kinds of teaching, and we can have something for all our students from many cultures. But what do I do? I try to find the science in the folktale. One idea I read about once in a professional book was to change the weather in a folktale. What would Gretel use (you know she was the one to be sure they had a trail of crumbs) if it was windy? What would Cinderella do if there was a thunderstorm (this was the one I read about)? The teachers who try to look for trouble say that we should focus on teaching the real folktale—my point is that we need to do that, of course, and then more to make the students think critically about what they are reading. Maybe because of scientific inquiry, I am more interested in the afterthoughts than in enjoying a story just for the sake of the story.

Even when I am helping students check out books, I throw my science interest at them, and they tease me about it. They call me Ms. Taylor, the Science Lady, like the female version of Mr. Nye, the Science Guy. That's okay with me. Where I struggle is with books that I "booktalk"—lots of books that I read and I am a terrible actress. It is dreadful, in fact, I dread it. I just cannot change my tastes, and I don't want children to feel like they need to read what they don't like to read. And then there are Lexiles to configure, Accelerated Reader to support, pizzas for pages, 600 minutes and win a day at a theme park, something new all the time. I am just not feeling "readability," and it shows.

LET'S DISCUSS LITERACY AND READING

It is our colleagues in the classroom, reading teachers, reading specialists, and literacy coaches who teach our students functional reading literacy and continue to guide the development of our students as effective and strategic readers. We have a supporting role in that reading instruction by nature of our constant interactions with the contact between students and text. Our role might vary based on a story read-aloud or on guiding students researching endangered species, but there are core understandings about reading we support for improved achievement of all our students.

School librarians see students for all the years they attend a school, and they guide their development with reading engagement, motivation, and entry into the literacy club. The school library is a laboratory where the literacy habit is germinated. It is that magical place that exists between the classroom, the home, and the public library that has the potential for supporting, guiding, and helping students reach beyond their current lives and selves and enter new and greater vistas within the safety of the school. Finding a place for each student in this reservoir of stories and information and ideas respects the student for the "powerful literate" that he or she has the potential to become.

> Reading takes us away from home, but more important, it finds homes for us everywhere.
>
> Hazel Rochman, *Against Borders: Promoting Books for a Multicultural World,* 1993

Although reading comprehension strategies, vocabulary acquisition, and fluency are generally deemed of critical importance in the study of reading instruction, the International Reading Association (IRA) and National Council of Teachers of English (NCTE) have identified 13 core understandings about reading as a learned language behavior. These 13 understandings represent a summary of reading research on best practice in literacy instruction and reading promotion. Following each understanding is a support statement that relates to the role of reading instruction in the school library media program. However, each core understanding has a comprehensive body of research-based literature worthy of further study in order to learn how to implement, support, and nurture reading instruction:

1. Reading is a construction of meaning from text. It is an active, cognitive, and affective process. *To support reading as a purposeful sociocultural, cognitive, and linguistic process, instruction should help readers make sense of written language.*

2. Background knowledge and prior experience are critical to the reading process. *Opportunities to expand background knowledge are provided . . . through a variety of experiences, such as read-alouds, discussions during and following reading, independent reading, written response to what has been read, access to many books and other reading materials, and virtual field trips.*

3. Social interaction is essential at all stages of reading development. *Authentic discussion that includes the exploration of ideas in a true dialogue is central to the developing understandings of readers and writers.*

4. Reading and writing are reciprocal processes; development of one enhances the other. *Engaging learners in many combined reading-and-writing experiences leads to a higher level of thinking than when either process is taught alone.*

5. Reading involves complex thinking. *Instructional tools such as anticipation guides, advance organizers, and questioning strategies . . . demonstrate that reading is a meaning-driven process and that cognitive strategy instruction is essential for achievement of content-area learning goals.*

6. Environments rich in literacy experiences, resources, and models facilitate reading development. *When students have a wide variety of print materials, including classroom, school library, and community collections, such as in public libraries, their access to literacy experiences increases.*

7. Engagement in the reading task is key in successfully learning to read and in developing as a reader. *Reading instruction should include diverse texts and diverse opportunities to interact with texts, rather than be limited to certain materials and procedures.*

8. Children's understandings of print are not the same as adults' understandings. *Children who fail to see the very nature and purposes of reading are often those who are seen to be at risk of not learning to read successfully.*

9. Children develop phonemic awareness and knowledge of phonics through a variety of literacy opportunities, models, and demonstrations. *Literacy instruction for adolescents should focus on individual interests and use diverse reading materials.*

10. Readers learn productive strategies in the context of real reading. *Opportunities to interact with many types of texts, in tandem with explicit instruction in problem-solving strategies for making sense of each type of text, must be provided.*

11. Students learn best when teachers employ a variety of strategies to model and demonstrate reading knowledge, strategy, and skills. *Questioning is a vital element in the processes of reading, which also include the ability to predict, summarize, clarify, and build knowledge.*

12. Students need many opportunities to read, read, read. *Indicators of school library quality and public library use are significant predictors of reading comprehension scores.*

13. Monitoring the development of reading processes is vital to student success. *Students must learn to become critically aware of their own reading processes, that is, to become metacognitive, in order to support their development as competent, engaged, and effective readers* (Braunger and Lewis 2006).

If you consider that reading instruction is focused on where the student has come from and on what reading abilities he or she possesses and that the literacy habit focuses on where the student might go or who he or she might become, reading engagement is the bridge between these two shores. Engagement has many interesting facets to consider when striving to nurture developing readers. Reading researchers find that students who are not engaged, not motivated to read, do not benefit from reading instruction, regardless of how specifically directed to student needs. There is a documented decline in motivation for reading as students move from elementary to middle school grades. At the same time, research shows that building competence builds motivation, which increases reading achievement and leads to more reading. Reading engagement also seems to mitigate underlying factors, such as limited educational background in the family and low-income economic status (Braunger and Lewis 2006, 72). Clearly, reading engagement and motivation are areas school librarians need to embrace and promote to ensure the development of a literate and informed citizenry.

In an article published in *Reading Research Quarterly*, "Just Plain Reading": A Survey of What Makes Students Want to Read in Middle School Classrooms, reading researchers Ivey and Broaddus (2001) studied over 1,700 middle school students to learn what makes them tick (or not) as readers. The authors contend that pre-teens get an unfair shake in our society; that their likes, dislikes, and habits are defined by others; and that they are not often asked to identify their own reading characteristics. Although the study

> Will you come with me, sweet Reader? I thank you. Give me your hand.
>
> Howard Pyle, *The Merry Adventures of Robin Hood*, 1883

centered on classroom instruction, the results uncovered what students valued most as their main motivation for reading at school more than any other factors: (1) time spent in independent reading and teacher reading-aloud; (2) the act of reading rather than the social aspects or activities related to reading; and (3) the "quality and diversity of reading materials." The authors concluded that there are major issues related to access to alternative reading materials in the classroom and in the school.

Each of the three findings of the Ivey and Broaddus (2001) study fits into the school library program and reinforces a "something for everyone" approach. Too often we fall into the cliché of a narrowly defined collection and concentrate on novels and series

> We shouldn't teach great books; we should teach a love of reading.
>
> B. F. Skinner, American psychologist, 1904–1990

nonfiction, without giving other media the attention they deserve. Alternative reading materials that are responsive to student choice include print and online resources, primary and secondary sources covering local issues and global perspectives. We cannot think or develop our collections with too broad a mind toward a diverse selection of materials that support our curricula and our extracurricular programs. Authentic ethnic music; Jackdaws (www.jackdaw.com) that contain thematically based facsimiles; special interest youth magazines; programs from the local zoo; realia borrowed from museum educational programs; locally produced zines and student work available for circulation; and a speakers' bureau of community human resources all belong in our learning laboratories. Many additions to a traditional school library do not divert much in the way of funding but more than extend the impact for students who are seeking their own path to literacy.

> Outside of a dog, a man's best friend is a book. Inside of a dog, it's too dark to read.
> Groucho Marx, American comedian, 1891–1977

The role of the school librarian in reading is one that is continuing to reveal itself. It is clear from the understandings about reading that nurturing learners to read in a literacy-rich environment is a good starting point. Learning more about the reading needs of each of our students is the next best step. Continuing to view reading as a path toward literacy, as a mind-set that enlivens the life of the mind, truly respects our students as the readers, writers, and learners that they are now and the adults they have the promise to become.

REFERENCES

Ivey, G., and K. Broaddus. 2001. "Just plain reading": A survey of what makes students want to read in middle school classrooms. *Reading Research Quarterly, 36*(4), 350–377.

Meek, M. 1991. *On being literate.* Portsmouth, NH: Heinemann.

Smith, F. 1988. *Joining the literacy club: Further essays into education.* Portsmouth, NH: Heinemann.

QUESTIONS AND ANSWERS ABOUT LITERACY AND READING

1. I am more concerned about doing harm than good. I am an elementary librarian, and I am cautious about getting involved with students regarding reading and getting in over my head, especially someplace my colleagues do not think I belong.

Hopefully, students are in the process of developing their reading strategies in elementary school. You are involved in the development of their reading strategies whether you would like to think so or not. You help students select books; you help students read passages in difficult texts; you consider the students' reading ability before suggesting certain titles for research sources; you learn about your students' personal interests to suggest appropriate independent reading. You ask predicting questions. You ask, "How is it going?" You ask "after" questions. You discuss content that enhances comprehension. Perhaps you ask a classroom teacher for the vocabulary list so that you can reinforce the use and spelling of the words on the list. You do everything in your power to create a warm and inviting literacy environment that allows reading habits to develop and flourish. You *are* involved in the reading life of your students. If you have a specific concern about components of reading, such as fluency or motivation, do your homework. If you want to keep up on current trends in reading instruction, read the International Reading Association's *Reading Teacher* and/or *Journal of Adolescent and Adult Literacy.*

Perhaps there was a time when a librarian could help a student by suggesting a book, handing it to a student, and walking away with the conviction that it was the right book for the right child at the right time. If so, that was then, but that is not now. School librarianship is a contact sport, and we need to gear up to support reading instruction in all of its multiple dimensions.

2. I was a reading specialist, and I decided that I would rather work in the school library. I do not want to go back to the pain and difficulty of working with struggling readers; it was just not a good fit for me. I want to create fun programming and teach research using information literacy models, and I never want to hear about lexiles or diagnostics again.

You are fortunate to have the literacy background that you bring to your position. Surely when you were hired, the administration considered your professional experience a plus. And perhaps you embellished it yourself through the interview process. Now there might be more of an expectation on you than on another librarian who does not have your reading background. Focus on the positives; you are probably making subconscious assessments all the time, about your collection, about reading strategies that could be subtly employed, about programming that might be fun and beneficial to your struggling readers. Because you did not "fit" with the diagnostic aspect of reading, stay on the literacy side of enhancing the literacy-rich environment of the school library. Earmark funds to serve the most struggling readers. Purchase magazines and alternative reading materials in their interest and at their reading levels. Seek out high-interest/low-ability engaging nonfiction books. Develop display areas that encourage student participation by bringing artifacts from home. Bring in storytellers and local authors and illustrators for your programming throughout the school year. Commit to broadening the attraction of literacy for those who need the help the most—you will be serving your professional background, your responsibilities, and your goals.

READ MORE ABOUT LITERACY AND READING

Bush, G. 2005. *Every student reads: Collaboration and reading to learn.* Chicago: American Association of School Librarians.

   A companion to the 2004 AASL Fall Forum, *Reading to Learn*, this book includes contributions from Peter Afflerbach, Donna Ogle, and Stephen Krashen. Checklists of collaborative action steps for the school librarians to take are based on the reading scholars' contributions. Grades K–12 collaborative lesson plans, developed by participants, demonstrate collaborative and interdisciplinary planning strategies.

Krashen, S. D. 2004. *The power of reading: Insights from the research.* 2nd ed. Westport, CT: Libraries Unlimited.

   Krashen reviews reading research with a focus on the benefits of free voluntary reading (FVR) in opposition to direct instruction. According to Krashen, the pleasure of the reading habit leads to success in schooling and in life. Research is well documented, format is accessible, and content is useful for promoting independent reading programming.

Moreillon, J. 2007. *Collaborative strategies for teaching reading comprehension: Maximizing your impact.* Chicago: American Library Association.

Written for elementary school librarians, this book is useful for any school librarian interested in learning more about specific comprehension strategies and how to put into practice the "two heads are better than one" philosophy. Studying each strategy and application as they are accessibly described in Moreillon's book furthers understanding of our critical role in guiding readers in the school library media program.

CONNECT LITERACY AND READING TO 21ST-CENTURY LEARNERS

A powerful model for school librarians to open the door to the literacy club is the AASL Dispositions in Action. Certainly the pursuit of personal and aesthetic growth specifically recognizes the role of an appreciation for literature in 21st-century learners' lives (4.2.4). But the learner who poses questions, investigates answers, uses research skills with flexibility, and is persistent in pursuit of information (all 1.2; 2.2.1, 2.2.2, 2.2.3, 2.2.4) requires a disposition—not only of reading ability, but a disposition toward a literate and informed life. For these learners, divergent and critical thinking enhance reading-to-learn experiences, and expressing learning through the reading-writing connection is a meaningful representation that is at its best a transformative experience that leaves an inquiring mind wanting to know more. Using literacy skills in social learning situations encourages classmates to follow suit. Students will often unknowingly model leadership and social responsibility in group discussions, and solid teamwork practices when cooperative learning experiences are particularly well planned, engaging, and authentic (3.2.1, 3.2.2, 3.2.3).

Learning literacy habits and strategies from peers is invaluable, and the independent learning environment of the school library is the perfect setting to observe these dispositions in action. Employing instructional strategies are just a few specific examples of teaching toward literacy and reading dispositions within the school library media program. Strategies might include using stations with alternative materials available that are relevant to the lesson and organized by topic at each library table; jigsawing cooperative learning groups to share the leadership and confidence among all members of a group as they are each responsible for teaching their topic to the group members; creating a collection development student advisory board for input in both selection and deselection for the library collection; implementing book clubs and readers' choice activities and creatively celebrating literacy holidays; and posting or displaying student book reviews.

DISPOSITIONAL PROMPTS ABOUT LITERACY AND READING

1. My administration will not budge. Ever since we purchased one of the reading packages, there is more interest in reading, the students like getting the points, and the fact that the results may not lead to a love of reading is almost laughable to my principal. I have stopped discussing it, because we have a circular argument every time I try to talk about it. My whole budget is going toward purchasing only the books with quizzes. In fact, my principal has said that, if we did not have this reading program, it would be cheaper for him, so I should be happy that the school library is receiving the funding that he is budgeting for it. I have students who hate the quizzes; in fact, I think those are the students I would call the real readers. The poor readers don't like the quizzes because they don't want to have anything to do with reading books. I

think that the average readers dissociate the quiz and points from the act of reading. They are on a constant search for the correct answer. This all feels bigger than anything I can hope to conquer.

2. We have a situation where a teacher brought in a number of books in Spanish to donate to the library. I processed them and included them in the collection. Then I purchased a few, a very few, more titles in Spanish. Then I started to wonder about books in the other languages that our students speak. We do not have an adequate budget to begin with, and now I am confused about what language to buy my books in. One of the secretaries in the main office thinks it is terrible that we have any books in a language other than English and that we are doing our Spanish-speaking students a disservice. She says books in Spanish hold them back from improving their English. One teacher who is Eastern European said that her family would never want books in their language in a U.S. school and that they came to this country to be Americans and that English is the U.S. language. I did not know what I was getting myself into. I thought that the Spanish-speaking students would appreciate having just a few books in their own language. If I am hurting their developing literacy, should I remove the books? Exactly how should I explain that to them?

Chapter Six

Diversity

Each year, approximately one-third of all high school students drop out rather than graduate. Even though the reasons for school failure are complex and multifaceted, when researchers and school personnel predict who might be at risk for failure, they generally consider one of two factors. The first is diversity and such individual characteristics as ethnicity, low socioeconomic status, family structure, or disability. The second factor is school practices that inhibit learning, such as inflexible schedules, narrow curricula, rigid instruction, tracking, and low expectations. How can school librarians ensure that all children succeed?

REGGIE

From the start of the year, I have just been trying to figure things out. I don't really know what I am doing in the LMC. And now I see the assistant principal coming toward me with an older lady and a scrawny sack of sad by her side. The assistant principal (AP) is a normal-sized American woman, and she is towering over all of us. It seems that Abir has come to live with his auntie (who is not related, but from the same place somewhere around the world). Today is his first day at Jefferson Middle School and they are putting him in seventh grade. I am waiting to hear why I have to know all this. Auntie thinks that Abir is "mechanical," and the AP thinks that he needs someone to check in with at the beginning of the school day. I get it. I am a little mechanical guy, and so is Abir. He looks like he belongs in fourth grade, and he has yet to take his eyes off the floor.

I don't even know what I am supposed to be doing in this LMC job, and they are adding babysitting to it. I say that I could use the help, I smile weakly, the auntie looks grateful, the AP takes her back down the hall, turns her head, and winks at me, and there we are, two little mechanical sacks standing around with nothing to say. I tell Abir that my name is Mr. Lorenz, and I welcome him to Jefferson Middle School. I ask him where he is from, how long he has been in the United States, but his eyes never leave the floor, and he does not make a sound. I ask him to follow me into the LMC and give him a little tour. Enough for his first day, I take him to Ms. Robinson, his math teacher, and tell him to see me in the LMC tomorrow before school. Then I remember that I was going to plan a lesson around using Rubistar for the metro history fair. This district is rubrics-happy. Until anyone tells me differently, I am going to keep on teaching technology tools that I know. I cannot teach what I do not know. And now I have Abir, another job I do not understand. Maybe if I just have him fill the paper in the copier and the printers every morning that will satisfy everyone.

LET'S DISCUSS DIVERSITY

Although school populations have always been varied, and—after all, each student is individual and unique—diversity is a broad term in our educational lexicon to mean cultural and racial/ethnic origins, language, economic status, and learning challenges. The more dissimilar students are from the educational system's status quo and from the teachers in their classroom, the more they are likely to struggle. Most U.S. teachers are European Americans from middle-class backgrounds who speak only English (Banks et al. 2005, 237). Many of their students are ethnic minorities, live in poverty, speak a first language other than English. Villegas and Lucas (2002) conclude that "the consistent gap between racial/ethnic minority and poor students and their White, middle-class peers . . . is indicative of the inability of the educational system to effectively teach students of color as schools have traditionally been structured" (9).

In the past five decades, the federal government has stepped in to pass legislation in response to changing school populations and the growing number of at-risk students in order to force states and school districts to educate *all* students, regardless of ethnicity, socioeconomics, language, and learning challenges. Throughout these decades, some educators and members of the public have attempted to maintain the status quo—rather than reform schools to meet the needs of all students, but especially those who are "different" from the school's majority and most at risk (Jones and Zambone 2007).

> I have a dream that one day this nation will rise up and live out the true meaning of its creed: "We hold these truths to be self-evident, that all men are created equal."
>
> Martin Luther King, Jr., American minister and civil rights activist, 1929–1968

The first attempt to reform schools addressed the issue of ethnicity, or race. In 1954, the Supreme Court ruled, in the case *Brown v. Board of Education*, that segregation of public schools is "inherently unequal." In the following years, as states and school districts struggled with the concept of "inherently unequal" and resisted integration, President Johnson signed into law the *Civil Rights Act* of 1964, which gave teeth to the Supreme Court's ruling in *Brown v. Board of Education,* by prohibiting discrimination in voting, education, and the use of public facilities, and enforced the racial desegregation of schools.

In similar fashion, federal legislation was enacted to permit students with disabilities to attend public schools and receive an equal education. The first legislation to address the needs of special education was Section 504 of the *Vocational Rehabilitation Act* of 1973, which prohibited discrimination against people with disabilities in any program or activity that received federal funding. Soon thereafter, the *Education of the Handicapped Act* (EHA) of 1976 confirmed the right of children with disabilities to a free, appropriate, public education. Over the years, EHA has evolved into the *Individuals with Disabilities Act* (IDEA), which addresses problems specific to special education, such as the rights of due process, individualized education plans (known as IEPs), least restrictive environment, and an interdisciplinary team to conduct assessments and planning (Jones and Zambone 2007).

> We should all know that diversity makes for a rich tapestry, and we must understand that all the threads of the tapestry are equal in value no matter what their color.
> Maya Angelou, American poet

The most recent legislative attempt to address the continuing cycle of failure for many students regardless of race, ethnicity, family income, dominant language, or handicap is *No Child Left Behind* (NCLB), the 2001 revision of the *Elementary and Secondary Education Act,* which was signed into law on January 8, 2002. Some educators and members of the public complain about NCLB, IDEA, and *Brown v. Board of Education* rather than applaud their purpose, which is to ensure an equitable education for all children. The intent of these laws, despite how it feels some days, is not to make things more difficult but represent an ongoing effort to reverse the failure of at-risk students.

When the educational system does not "work" for students, they are likely to disengage, drop out, and become part of the growing underclass. The term "demographic imperative" is used to state the rationale for everyone taking action to alter the disparities in opportunities and outcomes deeply embedded in the U.S. educational system (Banks et al. 2005).

> If we cannot now end our differences, at least we can make this world safe for diversity.
> John Kennedy, 35th president of the United States, 1917–1963

> The argument for the demographic imperative usually includes statistics about the increasingly diverse student population, the still relatively homogeneous teaching force and the "demographic divide" (Gay and Howard 2000, 1), especially the marked disparities in educational opportunities, resources, and achievement among student groups who differ from one another racially, culturally, and socioeconomically. (Banks et al. 2005, 236)

School librarians are morally obligated, as are all educators, to follow educational laws to ensure that *all* students achieve by providing appropriate learning opportunities.

The most important characteristic we bring to the "demographic imperative" is the quality of our teaching. An analysis by Ronald Ferguson found that teachers' expertise, defined as scores on a certification examination, master's degrees, and experience, accounted for more of the variation in students' reading and mathematics achievement in grades 1 through 11 than the student's socioeconomic status. These effects, along with teacher experience, were so great that, after controlling for socioeconomic status, the large disparities in achievement between black and white students were almost entirely accounted for by difference in teacher qualifications (Ferguson 1991, 9).

Variety is the spice of life.

American proverb

The Colorado impact studies, conducted by Keith Curry Lance, Marcia J. Rodney, and Christine Hamilton-Pennell and revised and repeated in many other states, indicate that students' academic performance improves when school librarians plan and collaborate with classroom teachers, develop and manage quality collections, and cooperate with other types of librarians, especially public librarians. In addition, academic performance improves when the school library is staffed by a professional school librarian and support personnel, information technology extends the reach of the school library into classrooms and labs, and a well-organized and formally requested budget is allocated (Lance 2002). The impact studies complement Ferguson's findings that teaching matters and make the case for competent and well-trained school librarians.

There is no magic bullet, but, through leadership and collaboration, we *can* provide an environment in which all children thrive. Consider the following strategies as you seek ways to implement the "demographic imperative" at your school:

- Effective school librarians link learning to students' experiences by maintaining connections with their students within their social contexts. They know their students. Effective teachers are familiar with community speech patterns and incorporate these patterns into teaching by focusing on the whole child and exhibiting the disposition that all children learn and succeed. The *Association for Supervision and Curriculum Development* has "launched a public engagement and advocacy campaign to encourage schools and communities to work together to ensure that each student has access to challenging curriculum in a healthy and supportive climate" (from the ASCD Web site at www.wholechildeducation.org/about). Providing a supportive and warm school librarian and an instructionally sound and engaging library is consistent with our profession's standards and expectations.

- Effective school librarians utilize exemplary teaching strategies, such as modeling, demonstrating, explaining, writing, giving feedback, reviewing, and emphasizing higher-order skills (AASL 2009). They differentiate instruction so students learn best. One framework for improving academic achievement is Marzano, Pickering, and Pollock's (2007) synthesis of research regarding the general factors that influence student achievement.

- How do you describe a school librarian disposed towards diversity? In Gay's (1993) words, he or she is a "cultural broker" who "thoroughly understands different cultural systems, is able to interpret cultural symbols from one frame of reference to another, can mediate cultural incompatibilities, and knows how to build bridges or establish linkages across cultures that facilitate the instructional processes" (293). We are bridge builders. In Chapter Eight on Communication, you will learn about the relational dispositions of bridge builders.

REFERENCES

American Association of School Librarians. 2009. *Empowering learners: Guidelines for school library media programs.* Chicago: American Library Association.

Banks, J., M. Cochran-Smith, L. Moss, A. Richert, K. Zeichner, P. LePage, L. Darling-Hammond, H. Duffy, and M. McDonald. 2005. Teaching diverse learners. In *Preparing teachers for a changing world: What teachers should learn and be able to do*, eds. Linda Darling-Hammond and John Bransford, 232–274. San Francisco: John Wiley.

Ferguson, R. F. 1991. Paying for public education: New evidence on how and why money matters. *Harvard Journal on Legislation 28*(2), 465–498.

Gay, G. 1993. Building cultural bridges: A bold proposal for teacher education. *Education and Urban Society 25*(3), 285–299.

Jones, J., and A. Zambone. 2007. *The power of the media specialist to improve academic achievement and strengthen at-risk students.* Worthington, OH: Linworth.

Lance, K. C. 2002. Impact of school library media programs on academic achievement. *Teacher Librarian 29*(3), 29–34.

Marzano, R. J., D. J. Pickering, and J. E. Pollock. 2001. *Classroom instruction that works: Research-based strategies for increasing student achievement.* Alexandria, VA: Association for Supervision and Curriculum Development.

Villegas, A. M., and T. Lucas. 2002. *Educating culturally responsive teachers: A coherent approach.* Albany: State University of New York Press.

QUESTIONS AND ANSWERS ABOUT DIVERSITY

1. My elementary school library is run on a fixed schedule, and I don't have an assistant. I teach six classes a day. I barely have time to do anything but herd students in, teach a lesson, and herd them out. I used to call roll before each class, but now I don't even do that. I stopped because I was mispronouncing so many of their names, and students would laugh and laugh. I really lost control of the class then. I know I can't go on like this, but I am not quite sure what to do.

   The starting point is always your students. The time you spend learning about their interests, goals, and strengths—and yes, the pronunciation of their names—is well worth your effort. You might consider making roll-taking into a more enjoyable experience by creating a research and cultural activity whereby your students research the meaning of names. In the chapter on dispositions, we referred to research conducted by Kathleen Cushman in which she asked high school students to describe the qualities of the teacher they most wanted. Students want to take engaging classes taught by teachers who care about the subject, to be treated as smart and capable of challenging work, and to be respected and cared for. Cushman has provided us with the recipe for making our classes count.

2. I am the school librarian in a middle school that is quite diverse. Every February we make a big event out of Black History Month. We do the same for Hispanic Heritage Month. I decorate the library and make nice book displays. Usually I am able to get extra funds to go "ethnic." Do you have other ideas for these months?

We should celebrate diversity every day. Everyone loves a celebration, so build more of this into your calendar. Another approach to recognizing and celebrating diversity is to select a monthly theme, such as sports, dance, science, history, food, toys, or music—and the list could go on and on. For each theme, identify the people, places, or things that help bring the topic to life. For instance, one month you might select toys of the world. Have students conduct research on toys. You could develop a display showcasing different types of toys and how these are used throughout the world—and even throughout history. Students could bring in toys to discuss. Run a competition to have students design a toy of the future for a particular culture that has been studied. Be as creative as you can to introduce students to the world. Ask your students what interests them and bring a global point of view to this inquiry.

READ MORE ABOUT DIVERSITY

Banks, J. A. 2001. *Cultural diversity and education: Foundations, curriculum, and teaching.* 4th ed. Boston: Allyn and Bacon.

This classic book is written by one of the leading scholars and researchers in the field of multicultural education. The book's five sections help readers understand the history and goals of multiculturalism, philosophical issues, knowledge construction and school reform, curriculum and teaching strategies, and gender, language, and intergroup relations.

Detailed report of the economic impact of the achievement gap in America's schools. 2009. http://www.mckinsey.com/clientservice/socialsector/detailed_achievement_gap_findings.pdf.

In this startling report, McKinsey & Company provides evidence that school performance and socioeconomic background are highly correlated in the United States and that performance is declining. In general, top-performing educational systems in other countries have smaller socioeconomic gaps in performance. Furthermore, socioeconomic achievement gaps are larger in the United States than in other countries.

Gay, G., ed. 2003. *Becoming multicultural educators: Personal journey toward professionals agency.* San Francisco: Jossey-Bass.

Gay, a multicultural leader and prolific writer, has edited a book of stories about teachers and their personal transformations to become multicultural educators. This work addresses "one of the most daunting tasks facing teachers today [which] is learning how to work with students from a wide range of ethnic, cultural, and social backgrounds."

CONNECTING DIVERSITY TO 21ST-CENTURY LEARNERS

In the 2009 report titled *Detailed Findings on the Economic Impact of the Achievement Gap in America's Schools,* the authors paint a startling picture of an educational system that cannot compete globally and is falling further behind each year. Students in Finland, Korea, Netherlands, and Canada score considerably higher on measurements of science and math than do U.S. students. Even more disturbing, school performance and socioeconomic background are more highly correlated in the United States than in many other countries. Our work is cut out for us. The goal of the AASL *Standards for the 21st-Century Learner* is to prepare students for a future we can only surmise; it is a world that none of us understands with total certainty—but we do know that *all* students must be prepared, which seemingly is not a strong suit of U.S. education. An emphasis on diversity requires school librarians to create engaging and rigorous learning opportunities for students to become "both divergent and convergent thinking to formulate alternative conclusions and test them against the evidence" (2.2.2) and to "display curiosity by pursuing interests through multiple resources" (4.2.1). We are to nudge students (as well as our peers) to "walk in another's shoes" by developing empathy, which is the capacity to understand the feelings, experiences, attitudes, and challenges of others. A variety of resources, including literature (4.2.4), are ideal to prepare our students to "respect the differing interests and experiences of others, and seek a variety of viewpoints" (3.3.2).

DISPOSITIONAL PROMPTS ABOUT DIVERSITY

1. Two Dispositions in Action in the AASL *Standards for the 21st-Century Learner* might be culturally inappropriate for the students living on the Warm Spring Indian reservation in Oregon. Disposition in Action 3.2.1 calls for students to "demonstrate leadership and confidence by presenting ideas to others in both formal and informal situations," and 3.2.2 asks them to "show social responsibility by participating actively with others in learning situations and by contributing questions and ideas during class." The incongruity for Warm Spring students is their reluctance to speak in class, which conflicts with their upbringing. At home, parents rarely ask their children questions or speak to them. Are these student dispositions culturally insensitive, or is it more important for them to learn to speak up?

2. Our school district is under a mandate from someone to hire teachers that have the same ethnic background as students. About 20 percent of students in this school district are Muslim and 15 percent are from Korea. It has become a huge issue locally in our district, as well as neighboring ones. I have been appointed to a committee to find ways to hire a more diverse teaching staff. Someone in our district office checked to see if there were Muslim or Korean undergraduate or graduate students studying to become teachers. The answer was no. At our next meeting, we are to bring ideas for discussion. I am stumped.

Chapter Seven

Intellectual Freedom
Carrie Gardner

Before opening my word processor to begin this chapter, I checked my e-mail. A common subject heading awaited me: book banned. The book in question is *My Sister's Keeper* by Jodi Picoult. Briefly, the plot involves a family that conceives a child in order to provide medical assistance to an already living child with a serious illness. As a kidney transplant is planned, the younger child decides she does not want her body used to help her older sister and hires a lawyer. A parent challenged the book, and the school board voted to remove it from the school library and ban its use by teachers.

Research shows that this scenario happens about six times a day every day in the United States. Challenges occur in public, academic, special libraries—but most often in school libraries. Why? We are a diverse society. We represent dozens of religions, speak over 200 different languages, and have different beliefs about sexuality, politics, abortion, medical ethics, capital punishment, creationism, evolution and every other topic in our world. Some look at our diversity as a positive aspect of society; others view it as a threat to their way of life, thinking, and world order.

DONNA

Stephanie teaches English, or Language Arts, if you will. Her mixed junior and senior classes have a high number of low-ability readers. To say that they are reluctant readers is an overstatement. Added to that equation is the fact that Stephanie insists that they read novels, not nonfiction, biography, or anything but full-length novels for the last quarter of the year. And Stephanie wants a booklist from me *and* for me to booktalk a collection of "edgy" books that would appeal to her students—not necessarily the books from the banned book list, because they seem tame compared to what Stephanie has in mind.

My creative solution to Stephanie's request is to have the youth services public librarian come to the LHS library and booktalk the "edgy" books they have in their collection. Frankly, that is where I think those books belong anyway. Teens seek out the edgy books and the comic books and the world records, etc. Our job in the school library is to introduce them to books and authors that they will not find on their own. My practical philosophy takes care of getting too close to that line that everyone is worried about. It is a simple division of spending for our collections based on the communities that we serve. The LHS collection has to be responsive to the curriculum; that is where our funding needs to be focused. I find the discussions about the latest, hottest books interesting—but not particularly relevant for our students. Our fiction collection is current, but it tends more to those books that are on our teachers' supplemental reading lists. Besides, what educator or parent does not agree that it is a good thing to have a close working relationship with our public library and to encourage our students to use their library cards for independent reading?

Needless to say, Stephanie is not offering that her department will help pay for these particular books, which I never had any intention of ordering. Maybe I should invite the school library liaison from the public library to meet with Stephanie one day during one of her prep periods. I think that they would get along famously; I would have made the connection, which is good collaborative practice, and the issue of ordering books that do not belong in our collection would have a neat and tidy resolution.

LET'S DISCUSS INTELLECTUAL FREEDOM

The American Library Association defines intellectual freedom in the following way:

[It is the] right of every individual to both seek and receive information from all points of view without restriction. It provides for free access to all expressions of ideas through which any and all sides of a question, cause or movement may be explored. Intellectual freedom encompasses the freedom to hold, receive and disseminate ideas.

American Library Association

But let us look at the question of intellectual freedom from a more practical point of view. We are school librarians. We interact with our students every day. We know their interests, their likes, dislikes, some of what is happening in their social lives and personal situations. On a day-to-day level, intellectual freedom means that school librarians provide what our student patrons want and/or need. No questions asked. No if, ands, or buts.

Fortunately, the law is on our side. In the United States, intellectual freedom has its basis in the First Amendment's Freedom of Speech clause. Numerous courts have declared that, in order for Americans to exercise the freedom of speech, they have the right to receive information. This is referred to as the *corollary* right to receive information and provides the legal underpinning for our profession. Furthermore, information in any format—books, videos, DVDs, music, and posters—is *legal* unless declared illegal by a court of law with appropriate jurisdiction.

Numerous court cases uphold the First Amendment right of minors to information. One of the most recent cases that went to trial was the book *Annie on My Mind* by Nancy Garden, depicting a lesbian relationship between two teenagers, which was removed from secondary school libraries in the Olathe, Kansas, school district in the early 1990s. In 1995, a Kansas court ruled that the removal of *Annie on My Mind,* based on disapproval of its ideology, violated the school district's own materials selection policy, as well as the First Amendment rights of students.

> Congress Shall Make No Law Respecting an Establishment of Religion, or Prohibiting the Free Exercise Thereof; or Abridging the Freedom of Speech, or of the Press; or the Right of the People Peaceably to Assemble, and To Petition the Government for a Redress of Grievances.
>
> U.S. Constitution, First Amendment

The Children's Defense Fund's Web site provides a realistic picture of the information needs and wants of U.S. youth based on their struggles and challenges. The 2009 data found at the Children's Defense Fund Web site tell us that each day in the United States the following actions take place:

- Five children or teens commit suicide
- Eight teens are killed by firearms
- Accidents result in 32 teenage deaths
- Teen mothers give birth to 1,154 babies
- There are 2,145 babies born without health insurance
- There are 2,467 high school students who drop out of school
- There are 2,421 children who are confirmed as abused or neglected
- There are 2,483 babies born into poverty
- Arrests include 3,477 children

Young people suffer physically and mentally when they do not have health care; go to bed hungry because their parents cannot afford food; are sexually, physically, and emotionally abused at the hands of other young people and adults; and have no place to live. The list of issues that have an impact on U.S. young people could fill this entire book. However, there are many young people who do not suffer any of the issues previously mentioned, but they attend school, play sports, engage in activities, and are friends with peers who do so also. Young people are not immune to the difficult issues that exist in our world. All young people have information needs that deserve answers. School librarians can and should provide answers in the form of information.

Regardless of students' informational needs and wants, dissension is a reality in a country that allows as much free speech as we have in the United States. Parents, teachers, administrators, community members, and organized groups have the right to challenge any information

> Libraries should challenge censorship in the fulfillment of their responsibility to provide information and enlightenment.
> ALA *Library Bill of Rights*

provided. And they do. The ALA's Office for Intellectual Freedom (OIF) maintains a database of all reported challenges. The top reasons for challenges include sexual content, homosexuality, offensive and sexually explicit language, age-inappropriateness, and violence. Approximately 35 percent of challenges originate from teachers, administrators, or other employees of the school district.

Patrons can face many types of barriers during their quest for information in a school library. One barrier is economic and includes any policy or procedure that requires patrons to pay for library services, resources, or programs. There are many documented cases of school library policies that require students to pay money before accessing online resources and, in some cases, the most popular books. Fees and fines, no matter how nominal they seem, can act as economic barriers to students who do not earn an allowance or paycheck or whose family's budget is stretched too thin.

A second type of barrier is physical—when resources are kept in areas of the school library that are off-limits to student patrons. When queried about this practice, school librarians often say they *know* the students who should "be allowed" to access certain resources and those who should not. With even the smallest school population, how can a school librarian know the personal, economic, and emotional issues faced by each student? A recent court

> I disapprove of what you have to say, but I will defend to the death your right to say it.
> Evelyn Beatrice Hall, *The Friends of Voltaire*, 1869—unknown

ruling in Arkansas found that an elementary school violated the First Amendment rights of patrons by enacting a policy that kept the *Harry Potter* books behind the circulation desk.

A third type of barrier is psychological—caused by policies and procedures requiring student patrons to interact with adults in order to receive information. They must overcome any embarrassment or annoyance they feel at having to request the item. All physical barriers pose psychological barriers for some student patrons.

Two policies assist librarians in the intellectual freedom arena in their school libraries—a resource selection policy and resource reconsideration policy. In order to carry the most legal weight, these policies must be approved by the school board and reaffirmed at least once every 10 years, but preferably every five years. Selection policies include sections that define the school library's philosophy on student access to information, the purpose of the collection, procedures for selection of resources, and a weeding policy. In virtually all states, legal responsibility for resource selection rests with either the school superintendent or school board and is delegated to school librarians.

Reconsideration policies provide information on how the school district formally reconsiders the inclusion of a resource in the school library or a classroom after a challenge. Sections include procedures on how reconsideration requests are handled and a form to use when filing a request for consideration. ALA's OIF provides an excellent resource for selection and reconsideration policy writing: the *Workbook for Selection Policy Writing.*

Whether you want to learn more about intellectual freedom or are experiencing a resource challenge, you are not alone. There are many organizations and individuals knowledgeable about this topic. The American Association of School Librarians (AASL) affiliate in virtually every state has intellectual freedom committees staffed by member volunteers. The AASL maintains a list of Web sites with links to the affiliates (AASL List of Affiliate Organizations). Staff members employed by State Library Agencies are often well-versed on state laws specific to governing access to information via libraries. Likewise, the ALA has created a number of documents, such as its *Code of Ethics,* about the legal aspects and the ethical implications of providing information to patrons of all ages. ALA's OIF is staffed by six full-time employees, including a lawyer, who stand ready to help anyone who contacts them. The caller need not be a member of ALA to receive assistance. Indeed, you are not alone.

> God forbid that any book should be banned. The practice is as indefensible as infanticide.
>
> Dame Rebecca West, English author, journalist, and literary critic, 1892–1983

REFERENCES

American Association of School Librarians. *AASL List of Affiliate Organizations.* http://www.ala.org/aasltemplate.cfm?section=affiliateassembly&template=/cfapps/aasl/affiliateassembly/directory.cfm.

American Library Association. *Code of Ethics.* http://www.ala.org/ala/aboutala/offices/oif/statementspols/codeofethics/codeethics.cfm.

American Library Association. *Workbook for Selection Policy Writing.* http://www.ala.org/ala/aboutala/offices/oif/challengesupport/dealing/workbookselection.cfm.

Children's Defense Fund Web site. http://www.childrensdefense.org/site/PageServer?pagename=research_national_data.

QUESTIONS AND ANSWERS ABOUT INTELLECTUAL FREEDOM

1. I think I had a lesson on intellectual freedom during library school, but now I'm a school librarian and facing some of these issues. My community is just like so many others in the United States. It's just me—I don't have an aide. I'm always behind at work, but I think I need to know more about intellectual freedom. Where do I begin?

   My hat is off to you. It's great that you understand the importance of intellectual freedom to your students. First, let me suggest that you surf the ALA OIF Web site at www.ala.org/oif. It is chock full of discussion points, sample policies, relevant court cases, and lists of people who stand ready to help in any way they can. But on a more practical level, all you have to do is think about the information your students need for their studies and want for their personal growth and development and start providing it. Survey them and buy the fiction they want to read. Respect their privacy and do not divulge how they use the library. Hold book groups using books that have been challenged and banned in schools just like yours. Celebrate Banned Books week at the end of September every year. Most important, support intellectual freedom for your students!

2. I know what my students want. I see the books they have checked out from the public library and bought at the bookstore. But I'm afraid to put them in my collection.

First, I applaud your knowledge of what your students want and need to read. With all respect, it's not your collection. It is there for your students. I understand why you would be fearful or concerned about what could happen if you provide certain kinds of information to your students. Some librarians are afraid of losing their jobs. Others worry about being labeled as a librarian who would provide *that* kind of information to impressionable kids; still others worry that the students will use information in some kind of harmful way. Let's tackle all of these. First, it is extremely rare for a librarian to be fired because he or she has provided books to young people, because, in virtually all states, it is not legal to fire someone over that type of issue. *If* you are fired for supporting intellectual freedom, there is a fund to support you until you find another job. You can learn more about this fund at http://www.ala.org/ala/mgrps/othergroups/merrittfund/merritthumanitarian.cfm. And you will find another job. But, again, I don't think you are going to be fired for providing books and other information to your students. There is not one piece of information that everyone agrees is good or bad for your students. No matter what books you provide, there is someone who feels that it is bad or inappropriate. Most librarians accept that fact, take a deep breath, and buy the books they want their students to have. No matter what label someone tries to apply to you, others will apply the opposite label. Lastly, students have been having sex, doing drugs, driving too fast, failing tests, and getting into all kinds of trouble since the beginning of time, and some students will do those things regardless of the books in the library.

READ MORE ABOUT INTELLECTUAL FREEDOM

The ALA Office for Intellectual Freedom Web site. 2009. http://www.ala.org/oif.

This Web site provides one-stop shopping for information about all aspects of intellectual freedom. Data on court cases, state privacy laws, federal laws, how to write solid library policies, questions and answers, and where to turn for help are easily located.

Chmara, T. 2008. *Privacy and confidentiality issues: A guide for libraries and their lawyers.* Chicago: American Library Association.

Chmara, one of the most respected First Amendment lawyers in the United States, wrote this seminal book that explains the importance of privacy to library users and how school librarians can create policies and procedures that obey all applicable laws and still allow the library to function.

Doyle, R. P. 2007. *Banned books: 2007 resource guide.* Chicago: American Library Association.

Published every three years, this resource guide lists all the public challenges to resources since ancient Greece. Included are ideas about how to celebrate Banned Books Week and how to educate others about intellectual freedom.

American Library Association, Office of Intellectual Freedom. 2006. *Intellectual freedom manual.* 7th ed. Chicago: American Library Association.

This is the bible of intellectual freedom. Produced by the Intellectual Freedom Committee and the ALA OIF, it contains everything one needs to know about what intellectual freedom involves, court cases, philosophical documents, and where to turn for help.

Reichman, H. 2001. *Censorship and selection: Issues and answers for schools.* 3rd ed. Chicago: American Library Association.

The sticky issue of self-censorship is discussed in this classic volume by Reichman. Perhaps the best section, "What do we do if . . . ," provides practical, boots-on-the-ground advice for school librarians faced with an intellectual freedom issue.

Scales, P. 2009. *Protecting intellectual freedom in your school library.* Chicago: American Library Association.

Scales, a retired school librarian and intellectual freedom advocate, produced this work on behalf of the ALA OIF committee. It provides useful information about intellectual freedom, minors, and school libraries.

CONNECT INTELLECTUAL FREEDOM TO 21ST-CENTURY LEARNERS

Antoine de Saint-Exupéry wrote: "*I know but one freedom and that is freedom of the mind.*" This sums up how one can define intellectual freedom—that, as humans, we have a right to think as we see fit and to the information we need to make up our minds. But let's move away from the philosophical and onto the practical. The four AASL Standards for the 21st -Century Learners state that learners use skills, resources, and tools to do the following:

1. Inquire, think critically, and gain knowledge;
2. Draw conclusions, make informed decisions, apply knowledge to new situations, and create new knowledge;
3. Share knowledge and participate ethically and productively as members of our democratic society; and
4. Pursue personal and aesthetic growth.

It is an easy jump from these standards to the obligation school librarians have to provide information that our students want and need. They cannot and will not develop critical thinking skills, the ability to apply knowledge and pursue personal growth, unless they have access to information that allows these skills to be developed.

Often times, resources are not provided to young people because the adults in the school and/or community do not want to admit that the students have a need for the information. I was in high school during the Reagan years. I grew up with the *Just Say No!* to drugs campaign in my world. Interestingly, I studied all types of drugs—uppers, downers, pot, alcohol, you name it. I have vivid memories of my health teacher insisting that I demonstrate for my class the substances that cigarettes deposit in human lungs by making a cigarette "smoke" while stuffed in a wad of cotton. I am not sure I got an "A" on that project, but I learned the harmful effects of all types of drugs. You could not pay me enough to smoke a cigarette. I can still picture the yucky stuff on the cotton. And I stayed away from all drugs. I did not want to harm my body. I took controversial information, my own high school-aged brain, and made good choices. Today many librarians struggle to provide authentic information to young people because they fear the consequences. Yet our students will not achieve the standards unless they have the information for their brains to think about and school librarians willing to take the necessary steps in order to protect their access to that information.

DISPOSITIONAL QUESTIONS ABOUT INTELLECTUAL FREEDOM

1. Even though Disposition 1.2.4 in the AASL *Standards for the 21st-Century Learner* urges students to "maintain a critical stance by questioning the validity and accuracy of all information"—and I think it's a really necessary skill for my high school students—not everyone agrees, and it is getting ugly here. The suburban community in which I live and work includes students from all levels of the socioeconomic scale, but most are in the middle. My English and social studies teachers do a joint unit on the problems of democracy. I offered to buy books on white supremacy groups and freedom of speech because students love to talk about movie censorship, books, manga, music, and all that, and I think they would be interested in the issues of censoring speech of groups that most don't approve of. When I suggested it at our planning meeting, everyone thought I was crazy. They said, "How can you even think of allowing students access to *that* kind of information." Whatever *that* means. It seems I have stirred up a bee's nest in suburbia. Most faculty are against the idea, but some are for it, and now the teachers are in a heated debate. What should I do?

2. As a middle school librarian, I really want to stock manga and some of the great contemporary fiction on the library shelves. Two of the best books for teens I've ever read are John Green's *Looking for Alaska* and *An Abundance of Katherines.* My students love to read about high school characters—and my eighth graders are only a few months away from being high schoolers themselves, so I don't understand all the fuss. Some of the teachers have made comments to me about manga and fiction. I haven't had any challenges yet, but, if I buy manga, I think it's just a matter of time. What should I do to prepare for the inevitable?

Section Three

Standing Up for What You Believe

Chapter Eight

Communication

Communication may seem a simple matter of uploading a page or two to a Web site, hanging a poster on the door of the school library, or e-mailing reminders to all your teachers about signing up for the book fair, but the vehicle is less important than the human dynamics of it all. The essence of communication is relationships. Sometimes we will float an idea (albeit, we think, a great one) by our teachers before doing our "homework" and wonder why our ideas— "Wouldn't flex scheduling be great?" or "Let's start a children's literature reading group" as described in the following tale—are not embraced more enthusiastically. Communication is *the* vital disposition for leadership, advocacy, collaboration, and most everything else we do.

LISA

Dr. Kelly runs a tight ship, and everyone who stays at WES pretty much appreciates that. It is not always the friendliest of places, but it feels like everyone is really trying to do what they think is best for their students. There are a few teachers who were here before Dr. Kelly was named principal (she taught at another school in the district before she was "Dr."), and they have their own opinions. History runs deep in schools, and sometimes you just have to know where the skeletons are buried.

For the most part, I have a good relationship with the teachers, although they are starting to feel like I don't know much about all the children's authors. On the other hand, I find that there is so much information online about award-winning books and lists of lists of children's books that I can usually always find what they are asking me about. It is just that I am not creative about using literature in the LRC.

I had an idea for the teachers to form this reading group, like a book group where we all read different new children's books, and that way they could help decide what we should order for the library. I decided to mention it casually at a faculty meeting right before the holidays. Oh man, that could not have been taken in a worse way. They thought that I was trying to get them to do my work for me—that, if I need to learn about new children's books, I should take a course in it and not bother them—they have plenty to do—and they asked if I would like to do some of their grading and lesson planning while they do my reading for me. I am still surprised by their strong negative reaction. Dr. Kelly did not say anything (this discussion all transpired over the refreshments table) but gave me a look that I could not read.

I wonder what happens at other elementary schools where there is a solo librarian. This kind of thing makes me rethink how I feel about my job. I do not know what went wrong. My sister-in-law thinks that sometimes I do not read signals from people the way other people do, that I do not connect to them in a natural way. Maybe I belong in a science lab, happily connecting to petri dishes and microscopes. I do need to figure this out, because I think that I should have good relationships with my teachers. My dad has this great baseball saying, "You win some, you lose some, and some get rained out, but you dress for them all." I have to figure this out.

LET'S DISCUSS COMMUNICATION

We are going to share a secret in this chapter that is not expressed often but—believe us—is discussed around the water cooler. When it comes to school libraries, teachers are not the bad guys, and neither are principals. School boards are not "out to get us." Whether the school library is a huge success or ho-hum is a consequence largely of the librarian's dispositions and skills. It *is* all about us. Our success does not stem solely from education or degree, but rather from the dispositions described in this book; and communication is the pillar for all we do.

In the medical field, the long-standing recognition that some doctors lack certain patient skills has fueled an interesting question: Can "bedside manner" be taught? "Bedside manner" is mostly about communication and problems in this area present themselves when the doctors do not listen, use words and concepts not easily understood by patients, and employ body language that relays the message "I am way too busy."

> When people talk, listen completely. Most people never listen.
> Ernest Hemingway, American writer and journalist and winner of the 1953 Pulitzer Prize for the *Old Man and the Sea* and the 1954 Nobel Prize for Literature, 1899–1961.

Doctors Weissmann, Branch, Gracey, Haidet, and Frankel conducted an experiment with 12 physician-teachers who met twice a month for 18 months to practice skills designed to enhance compassion. Afterward, these doctors outscored a control group on measures of listening to others, teaching communication skills to medical students and residents, and adopting caring attitudes toward patients. Weissmann et al. found that exemplary physician-teachers teach the disposition of care and communication primarily through role modeling. The following four aspects of modeling employed by the exemplary physician-teachers are especially relevant for school librarians:

- Nonverbal cues, such as listening, making eye contact, tone of voice, and pace of speech

- Demonstrating respect for their patients, by making proper introductions or asking the patient's permission before turning down the volume of the television or listening to requests of patients
- Building personal connection by finding shared interests
- Reflection and self-awareness of their treatment of patients

Some school librarians have poor "bedside manners," which limits their ability to influence others, collaborate, and provide quality service. School librarians struggling in this area could apply the findings of Weissmann et al. regarding the importance of utilizing nonverbal cues, respecting all constituents, building personal connections, and reflecting on your service and support to students, teachers, and administrators.

In 2007, Jami Jones, with the assistance of graduate students, conducted a survey of 250 18-to-24-year-olds in North Carolina to explore perception toward bookstores and academic, public, and high school libraries. For the most part, these emerging adults liked the laid-back atmosphere of the bookstore, appreciated the academic library as a place to study and spend time between classes, held fond memories of the public library's storytime programs they attended during childhood, and remembered the high school library mostly as a place to conduct that despised research project. Although some students expressed positive attitudes about the school librarian, the negative impressions, such as "mean," "controlling," and "rigid," far outweighed the positive ones. Obviously the messages some school librarians are communicating might not be the ones he or she wants to convey.

> To effectively communicate, we must realize that we are all different in ways we perceive the world and use this understanding as a guide to communicate with others.
> Anthony Robbins, American self-help author and speaker

According to research by Albert Mehrabian (1987), communication is less about words than about body language. He found that body language accounts for 55 percent of the message, tone of voice is 38 percent, and the content of words is a mere 7 percent. A staggering 93 percent of communication is nonverbal. Nonverbal communication consists of body language—such as gestures and postures, tone and intensity of voice, and facial expression and smiling. How we greet students as they enter the library or colleagues in the hall does matter because our reputation and the perceived quality and value of the library are intertwined. Even more interesting is the notion that actions speak louder than words. Mehrabian found that when verbal and nonverbal language conveys conflicting messages, people almost always tend to believe the nonverbal message, which is seen as a more reliable reflection of how the communicator actually feels.

What may be holding back some school librarians from making a "heart of the school" impact are the relational skills and emotional intelligence to manage a job that requires significant strengths in the dispositional areas of leadership, advocacy, and collaboration. Daniel Goleman (1995) focuses on emotional intelligence as an array of competen-

> "Who wants to be friends with someone who scowls all the time?" asked Mr. Fridley. "So you've got problems. Well, so has everyone else, if you take the trouble to notice."
> Beverly Cleary, Dear Mr. Henshaw, 1983

cies that drive leadership performance. His model of emotional intelligence outlined in the book of the same name consists of four categories:

- Self-awareness—the ability to read emotions and use gut feelings to guide decisions
- Self-management—the ability to keep one's emotions and impulses in check, adapt to changing circumstances, and reframe situations more positively
- Social awareness—interpersonal skills; abilities to sense, understand, and react to other's emotions; understanding social networks
- Relational management—employs empathy, ability to inspire, influence, and mentor others, manage conflict

If we can clearly sense the feelings and attitudes of others, we can relate to them in ways that respect and value their feelings and thereby ensure that our needs and wishes are clearly expressed in return. Serious misunderstandings can occur if we fail to interpret nonverbal messages correctly, or if we send nonverbal messages that do not accurately reflect our emotions. The ability to "speak" and to "listen" nonverbally allows us to interact with one another more effectively.

The book-learning part of our studies to become school librarians such as reference and cataloging is vital, but the relational, emotional, and communication skills to further the school library program by manag-

> Communication is the real work of leadership.
>
> Nitin Nohria, Professor of Business Administration and leadership expert

ing school politics, developing a program that inspires teachers and students, and intuiting needs are every bit as important. In a position such as ours, in which teachers and principals are not quite sure what we do anyway, relational dispositions rule—these tend to be highlighted when we are judged. Rather than drawing back like a turtle hiding in its shell, it is necessary for us to step out boldly, to communicate to our constituencies our role by crafting succinct messages and delivering these in ways that students, teachers, administrators, parents, and community members relate to, understand, and support.

> The single biggest problem in communication is the illusion it has taken place.
>
> George Bernard Shaw, Irish playwright and winner of the 1925 Nobel Prize for Literature and 1938 Oscar, 1856–1950.

A few quick Google searches on "what employers want from employees" finds, at the top of the lists, communication skills—such as strong writing, public speaking, conversation, listening, conflict resolution, and interpersonal skills—and the ability to get along with a variety of personalities. Some school librarians may need strengthening in this area—perhaps this disposition as it relates to libraries was never modeled, or the discussion about communication has never taken place. To this we reply that school librarians need their own version of the phenomenally popular book, *All I Need to Know I Learned in Kindergarten* by Robert Fulghum, which focuses not on academics, such as memorizing the alphabet and numbers, but on the relational basics of sharing, kindness, fairness, and holding hands while crossing the street, as well as the importance of the afternoon nap. Good advice for us all.

Until this book is written, a good starting point is to build our support group—one teacher and administrator at a time—by listening more than talking, knowing when to speak, extending kindness to everyone, developing clear messages free of library speak, and recognizing that "variety (as well as flexibility) is the spice of life."

REFERENCES

Fulghum, R. 2004. *All I need to know I learned in kindergarten.* New York: Random House.

Goleman, D. 1995. *Emotional intelligence: Why it can matter more than IQ.* New York: Bantam Books.

Mehrabian, A. 1987. *Silent messages.* Belmont: Wadsworth.

Weissmann, P., W. Branch, C. Gracey, P. Haidet, and R. M. Frankel. 2006. Role modeling humanistic behavior: Learning bedside manner from experts. *Academic Medicine 81*(7): 661–667.

QUESTIONS AND ANSWERS ABOUT COMMUNICATION

1. I totally understand how Lisa feels, because this happens to me too. I feel that I never quite express myself well enough to get people to understand what I mean. I have received that "Dr. Kelly look" (except my principal is Dr. Cook) on several occasions and it chills me to my bones. It seems that the most trivial things I say become an issue, and then I have to retrace my steps and apologize, which is a time-consuming process. I am smart and did well in school. As a matter of fact, I was at the top of my class in my graduate studies and received the award for being the school librarian most likely to achieve. So why am I having such a difficult time achieving?

   Communication is a separate set of dispositions and skills that does not relate to the "book learning" you describe. By the way, congratulations on your award! You can improve your disposition of communication by employing the three essential components of dispositional behavior described in Chapter One on dispositions: the sensitivity to recognizing the need to develop the disposition of communication; the inclination or tendency to want to communicate; and the ability or capacity to communicate relationally. The starting point for communication is relationships. Even though we talk to students, teachers, and administrators about the value of the school library—and upload Web pages, hang posters, and send e-mail reminders about the book fair—unless there is a relationship, our messages will not be heard.

2. I am in the middle of my graduate program to become a school librarian and don't understand why communication isn't taught more—really, at all. Although I haven't been in this profession long, I have seen several of my classmates fail miserably in jobs, even though they were smart. Why isn't communication part of the library school curriculum?

   This is a good question. Other professions are looking at the affective and relational qualities needed to do the job. Oftentimes we hear people talk about their doctor's lack of good communication skills, even though "he (or she) is such a good doctor," but researchers at two large U.S. medical centers found that patients put personal attributes such as bedside manner ahead of medical competence—as if understanding one's profession compensates for the inability to communicate because both are necessary. Some people confuse the characteristics of care, compassion, and communication with inborn traits that you either have or do not have. These qualities can be acquired through modeling—and we are believers that all dispositions can be learned. Library educators should consider the modeling, reflection, and development of interpersonal skills that would strengthen our profession.

READ MORE ABOUT COMMUNICATION

Collins, R., and P. J. Cooper. 1997. *The power of story: Teaching through storytelling.* Salem, WI: Waveland.

Collins and Cooper discuss the power of storytelling to empower educators and learners to communicate feeling, synthesize and verbalize personal experiences, and construct meaning.

Perkins, P. S. 2008. *The art and science of communications: Tools for effective communication in the workplace.* Hoboken, NJ: John Wiley & Sons.

Perkins provides a model for communication, with chapters describing the following types of communication: intrapersonal, nonverbal, interpersonal, small group/organizational, public, mass, and intercultural.

Kougl, K. 1997. *Communicating in the classroom.* Salem, WI: Waveland.

This well-organized and easy-to-comprehend book, written for teachers with little or no formal training in communications, is organized into three sections: understanding the communication process; the three building blocks of effective communication, which are nonverbal, verbal, and listening behaviors; and oral communication in the classroom.

CONNECT COMMUNICATION TO 21ST-CENTURY LEARNERS

Communication is a disposition not explicitly identified in the *AASL Standards for the 21st-Century Learner,* but its footprint is evident throughout. Three dispositions in action in particular speak to communications. For instance, "display initiative and engagement by posing questions" (1.2.1), "show social responsibility by participating actively with others in learning situations and by contributing questions and ideas during group discussions" (3.2.2), and "demonstrate teamwork" (3.2.3) each has its roots in communication. These dispositions require students, as well as school librarians, acting as role models to develop and practice components of communication such as social engagement, empathy, teamwork, and respect. These relational expectations begin with us because we are the models and communicators of the message that students are to act in caring, supportive, and respectful ways toward each other. We do this by developing assignments that involve authentic teamwork—not just "grade grubbing." We value and respect all student comments and input, regardless of their ethnicity, language preference, special need, or socioeconomic level. Creating information literacy activities in which no one group has the edge, but all are travelers on the same road of inquiry, is a starting point for building the disposition of communication.

DISPOSITIONAL QUESTIONS ABOUT COMMUNICATION

1. I interviewed for my first school library job and was shocked that the principal spent so much time asking me questions about my communication style. I was ready to discuss cataloging, information literacy, and collaboration, but I had not prepped for communication. I started blabbering about Web pages and how I was pretty fair with a desktop publishing program, but I could tell this is not wanted he wanted to hear. Communication wasn't even part of the "test," which, as a matter of fact, I aced. I am about to go on my second school library interview, and I am really worried what I might be asked this time and whether it has anything to do with school librarianship. What does a school librarian need to know, and where does communication fit in?

2. I started working at a school several years ago, and the principal is always telling us that we are one family. I agree that it is important to get along and work together for the good of the cause, but a family? No way. I am trying hard to forget the dysfunctional family I grew up in. What is my principal really saying when he encourages us to act as a family?

Chapter Nine

Advocacy
Gail K. Dickinson

The best part of being a school librarian is that no one truly knows what our job is. That gives us the freedom to set our own goals, based on national guidelines and standards, along with best practices of the field. We can teach butterflies one period and digital storytelling the next. We can help the ninth graders recreate Pickett's Charge at the battle of Gettysburg in the morning and work with advanced placement seniors on research topics in the afternoon. It is an exciting whirl of projects, planning, and, for most school librarians, the most fun job in the world.

The worst part of being a school librarian, though, is that no one truly knows what our job is. We hear comments such as "So, do you really need a master's degree to do that?" or "It must be nice to sit in the back room and read books all day." More serious is the evidence that parents, admin-

> Libraries are at the heart of the learning experience for almost 44 million elementary, middle and high school students in schools with library media centers.
> U.S. Department of Education

istrators, and state and national decision makers do not understand the job, which happens when our requests for funding and sometimes even school library positions are cut. The solution to these problems is advocacy.

REGGIE

A few times a year my consolidated (K–12) district holds institute days and the "library department" meets. The high school librarian takes charge. Patrick is a great older guy, who has been at the school forever, and everyone loves him. The library is comfortable but used pretty much like a study hall. The elementary librarians are just overworked, period; their time is total prep time for the teachers. I remember trying to teach them how to use Rubistar, and you would think I was teaching them how to play bridge in outer space. I am the new guy in the library department, and, in a way, sometimes that is a good thing.

At these meetings, the usual talk is about budget and data-bases and problems with the circulation system and how to collect statistics. I have attended only two meetings, but they could have been interchangeable except for the refreshments (based on the closest upcoming holiday). We have another meeting coming up next month.

Maybe Abir has gotten me to think about it, but I thought that it might be fun to have tech clubs at all our schools—we could give them different but related club names and kind of build the skills and responsibilities needed to be in the club. That way the students in the elementary tech club could look forward to being in the middle school club and then the high school club—not that they would have to, but the option would be open to them. I would have liked that if it had been available in my schools. I know I am prejudiced, but I think it is a brilliant idea. On the other hand, I do not know how to talk about it with my library department. It will work best if we could get some funding and support like other clubs and teams, and this is starting to feel completely over my head.

I have always attended these local mini-conferences with technology teachers from around the area. It turns out that we have a mix of school librarians and tech teachers in our organiza-tion (I never noticed that before). Some of the other schools have tech clubs, so I asked them how they got started. The more they talk, the more I realize something. This is just like me; I don't really know much about what I am supposed to be doing, but I want the kids to have fun. I am mixed up on the how, who, when, and what of this idea, but I still like the why of it. And suddenly I realize that it is time for my performance review to be sched-uled with the AP and I wonder about tabling the club idea until I have a better handle on the library end of things.

LET'S DISCUSS ADVOCACY

Advocacy can be defined as a planned series of actions to advance the library program with an identified group of supporters. This definition, especially the last part, separates advo-cacy from either public relations or marketing, although it has elements of each. Advocacy is not just blanket promotion of the library program, and it is not merely selling the concept of the school library. Advocacy involves planning, target groups, strategies, and assessments.

- Planning: An advocacy plan is generally led by the school librarian, but it is devel-oped in coordination with an identified group of supporters, usually the library advi-sory committee at the school. The advisory committee often consists of several class-room teachers, an administrator, a few parents, and students, if appropriate. The advisory committee is the policy board for the library, so it is appropriate for the advocacy plan to be developed at this level. The advocacy plan is long-term, usually three to five years, and is based on the mission statement of the school library program. It identifies the overall goal of the advocacy plan, the target groups, the strategies, and the assessments that will be used to determine progress.

- Target Groups: The old adage that all politics is local remains true. The target groups must be within the grasp of the advocacy plan. In general, target groups are parents or the local taxpaying community, school faculty, administrators and school boards, and legislators.
- Strategies: Although individual strategies should be designed for each of the target groups, the overall purpose should fit under the umbrella of the overall advocacy goal. The analogy most commonly used is that of an advocacy train. There may be different cars, all with

> Be strategic, focus, and don't scatter your energies on many things that don't add up to a better whole.
> Marian Wright Edelman, Advocate and founder of Children's Defense Fund

different cargo, but the train is linked to the engine, and all cars are running in the same direction on the same track. If that doesn't happen, disaster is sure to follow. Strategies must be achievable in the light of all of the rest of the work of the library program and should not all be under the direct action of the librarian. The school librarian has limited time, limited energy, and limited money. Remember that the goal is long-term, so the strategies should be designed so that the stamina of the supporters is maintained. Having a major reading celebration once each semester is enough. Planning for one a month may not be achievable, even if the responsibility for planning it is delegated. Even the enthusiasm of the most dedicated supporters can be daunted over time.

- Assessments: Assessments must be measurable and must relate back to the goals. One of the most commonly used assessments is funding, especially when directed to administrators. If the advocacy effort is successful, the library budget will increase or be held harmless in difficult economic times. Advocacy goals and measures are sometimes confused. If increased funding is an assessment measure of an advocacy goal, it cannot also be the goal. It sometimes helps to first identify the target groups and then, for each, to brainstorm two questions with the planning committee:

1. I want this group to . . .
2. I can tell how much they are achieving this goal by . . .

> When I read about the way in which library funds are being cut and cut, I can only think that American society has found one more way to destroy itself.
> Isaac Asimov, Russian-born American author of science fiction, 1920–1992

For instance, if one of the advocacy goals is to create an understanding of the purpose of the school library in the school, and the target group is the principal, one of the measures could be to assess the number of times that the library facility was used for nonlibrary purposes. As the principal's understanding grows, the uses of the library for testing, health screenings, or senior pictures, for example, should decrease. Another assessment may be funding, but both of these assessments fall under the umbrella of increasing direct support of the library.

Advocacy, although it has been called by many different names, has been with the library field since the beginning. Advocacy is part of the job of the school librarian. The lack of understanding of the value of school libraries to the educational program of the school can be seen as our greatest problem. For a field based on collaborative relationships and open access to resources and materials, the lack of understanding of what the school librarian does all day is indicative that it is a part of that job we just have not done very well.

There is good news, however. First, we do have small numbers of passionate supporters. As Hartzell (2004) points out in his book *Building Influence for the School Librarian: Tenets, Targets, and Tactics,* no one really hates us, belittles us, or is actively campaigning against school libraries. As a field, we are just ignored and invisible. Only we can change that. We can work to increase the number of our supporters, and we can organize them to involvement in an advocacy program on several levels to portray our true worth.

Remember as well that advocacy doesn't just benefit school libraries. Strong school libraries mean students are learning more, differently, and better than they did before the advocacy efforts. Teachers are teaching more

> The highest achieving students come from schools with good library media centers.
> Keith Curry Lance, Marcia J. Rodney, and Christine Hamilton-Pennell, *How School Librarians Help Kids Achieve Standards,* 2000

effectively. Administrators are stretching dollars to benefit every student in the school through the school library, and legislators are seeing test scores rise as schools benefit from stronger school libraries.

REFERENCES

Hartzell, G. 2004. *Building influence for the school librarian: Tenets, targets, and tactics.* 2nd ed. Worthington, OH: Linworth.

QUESTIONS AND ANSWERS

1. I feel so embarrassed when I talk about the school library. Funds are short, and everyone is asking for extra money, and there is so little to go around. I am afraid that I will be seen as just another educator out for a handout. Sometimes when I see school board members at the grocery store or in church, I would like to talk to him or her about my school library. Is it alright to talk about school library issues at these times?

    Advocating for the school library is simply standing up for what you believe and helping the target audience to understand its importance to the academic, social, and emotional well-being and development of students. What school leader does not want this for students? We perform a wonderful and unique service in the school that some school and community leaders may not realize. They may never have been approached with a concise and focused message about the power of the school librarian. Sometimes school librarians will vent among themselves about a myriad of problems, such as the loss of funding or the uncertainty of the program, but the better way to deal with these problems is to plan an advocacy campaign in which school administrators and leaders learn about the impact of school librarians. The first step is to become an expert about the impact of school libraries by reading information available at the AASL *Advocacy Toolkit* and familiarizing yourself with the Impact Studies available at http://www.lrs.org/impact.php. You must understand and communicate the importance of school libraries. The second step is to communicate to school board members the importance of school libraries by developing a short, effortless, and informational "elevator speech" to deliver at a moment's notice whenever and wherever the opportunity arises.

2. What if my advocacy efforts do more harm than good? I hate to stand out and bring attention to myself, especially now during these tough economic times when administrators are looking for every opportunity to get rid of individuals and programs. It seems to me that some people are more popular than others, and their programs always receive full funding. What is their secret? What if people get upset with me? I understand the importance of advocating for the school library, but I think that doing a good job should be good enough.

Doing a good job is commendable, but not good enough. Come to think of it—it never really has been, but especially not now. Some of your colleagues may find it easier to speak out because their personality is more extroverted, but anyone can become an advocacy expert. We consider advocacy to be a disposition of the school librarian, because it is essential to educate others about our value if the library is ever to become the "heart of the school," which is our aim, after all. Even though school librarians have always struggled to be recognized and have their programs funded, we are in a unique position to improve the learning environment for students, because the skills we teach, such as finding and evaluating information, and the dispositions we model, such as displaying initiative and curiosity, are vital at a time of great change and information overload. It is precisely these skills and dispositions and those in the AASL *Standards for the 21st-Century Learner* that students need in order to compete globally. Educators and administrators may be myopic about the value of the school library program and information literacy—and continue to be this way—unless we share our enthusiasm and knowledge with them. It is our responsibility through advocacy to enlighten the educational community about the impact of school libraries.

READ MORE ABOUT ADVOCACY

Hartzell, G. 2004. *Building influence for the school librarian: Tenets, targets, and tactics.* 2nd ed. Worthington, OH: Linworth.

Hartzell has written a clear how-to guide for promoting the school library. Part One outlines the tenets of influence and provides a general understanding of the nature and operation of workplace influence, with particular attention to what these principles and theories imply for school librarians. Part Two zeros in on specific influence targets in the school, their importance, and ways to capture their support. The final section offers a small collection of influence-building and influence-enhancing tactics specifically addressing elements of school librarians' work lives.

American Association of School Librarians. 2009. *Advocacy toolkit.* http://www .ala.org/ala/mgrps/divs/aasl/aaslproftools/toolkits/aasladvocacy.cfm.

The AASL @your library® campaign seeks to increase public awareness of the significant contributions of school librarians to the academic, social, and emotional well-being of students. The *Advocacy Toolkit* provides school librarians with concise and focused talking points to deliver—to school officials, parents, and community members—the information needed to develop an effective advocacy campaign. Be sure to browse the entire site, which includes the AASL statement on instructional classification, slideshows on strategic marketing for school libraries and advocacy training, and many other helpful resources.

CONNECTING ADVOCACY TO THE 21ST-CENTURY LEARNERS

The ability to advocate for causes that are important not only to you and to the well-being of the school library, but it stands as an example to students who, throughout life, will be faced with situations requiring action and the dispositions and inclination to plan strategically for change—whatever that change might be. Students exhibit dispositions and behaviors to advocate for programs, services, or ideals when they "display initiative and engagement by posing questions and investigating the answers beyond the collection of superficial facts" (1.2.1), as well as when they demonstrate confidence (1.2.2), creativity (1.2.3), and emotional resilience to persist (1.2.6), because the first step is to understand the advocacy issue, followed by having the confidence, creativity, and persistence to carry on. The dispositions necessary for advocacy are developed and strengthened when school librarians create rigorous learning opportunities for students to "demonstrate leadership and confidence by presenting ideas to others in both formal and informal situations" (3.2.1) through debate or clubs. Students who are provided learning opportunities that require them to "maintain openness to new ideas by considering divergent opinions, changing opinions or conclusions when evidence supports the change, and seeking information about new ideas encountered through academic or personal experiences" (4.2.3) acquire the dispositional "habit of mind," which is the critical thinking that becomes second nature when individuals are confronted with problems or changes to be made.

DISPOSITIONAL PROMPTS ABOUT ADVOCACY

1. I am not naturally a pushy person. As a matter of fact, I am pretty quiet. I went into school librarianship because I wanted to work with children, and I thought the pace of the school library better would suit me better. Recently a new school board was voted in on a platform of cost savings, and now almost every program and service is under scrutiny, but the school libraries could be in trouble. We have never promoted ourselves or done anything very remarkable. We have good solid school libraries, attractive environments, and seem to be doing a good job of serving students and

teachers, but we are not as showy as other parts of the school system. I happened to miss the last monthly school librarian meeting, and now I find myself voted in as chair of a new committee to start advocating for libraries. Besides reminding myself never to miss another meeting, what do I do now about advocating?

2. I understand the importance of advocacy. I have always felt that if you do not toot your own horn, who else will? I work with teachers who are restrained, and I feel that I am going overboard because I am strategically planning to get my message out about the school library. Maybe I am too over the top. What is a disposition of advocacy? What does that mean and how should I be acting?

Chapter Ten

Collaboration

Ask school librarians if they collaborate, and you will receive a range of responses, from "Who has the time?" "Do you know what my day is like?" to "Of course, the teacher teaches the unit, and I demonstrate the databases." One reason for this curious spectrum, which does not answer the basic question, is in part fundamental to the nature of collaboration. Another suggestion relates to a defensive stance from our colleagues, who, having read the professional literature, understand the concept, and yet feel guilt or regret at not seeking out collaborative relationships. A brief description of the phenomenon might help us parse out what our friends in the business field call "true collaboration."

DONNA

Over the holidays, I had time to reflect back on this school year so far. I started thinking about how I have been handling things in the LHS library lately. For some reason, my initial response to everything (at least in the last few years) seems to be to duck or to wait patiently for a new trend to pass, and, when the coast is clear, I resurface with a new book display and a snazzy bulletin board. That is not how I handle things in my personal life, as a wife or mother, and so it is curious to me that this is who I have become professionally. Something has to change; I have been in the world long enough to know that the something may be me.

On the other hand, I am not a pushover. I do not mind pulling books for a teacher and putting them on a cart for his or her classes, even though it seems ridiculous that the students could not do it themselves. Oh, but locating resources is not the focus of our lesson. Well, it better be one of these days, or these students will leave high school never actually having had to go to the library shelves to find resources. Their college librarians will not be so accommodating, nor will every public librarian they encounter.

So when Jenn (special education) and Marta (world history), who teach resource classes together, came to me and wanted to plan a lesson, my immediate response was to wonder what they think I would do for them so that they would not have to do their own work. I did not say anything, but that was honestly what I was thinking. Why do I think that way? Why not be happy that teachers want to collaborate with me, when most school librarians are bemoaning the fact that their teachers don't want to have anything to do with them?

We planned to meet during the last period of the day the following Wednesday. Jenn brought her concerns about students feeling that research is for other students but not for them, and Marta suggested that we start with students researching the history of their family's country of origin. Jenn was going to survey her students on their favorite and least favorite parts of research, and Marta is going to have the students talk to their families and select the nation of their heritage (Marta thinks that it should be a family decision, because, in some cases, it is a delicate issue). I said that for the next meeting I would research relevant Web sites with appropriate reading levels and match our collection against the list of nations provided by Jenn. Now it will be interesting to see who follows through. So small, so friendly, so far so good.

LET'S DISCUSS COLLABORATION

The phenomenon of educator collaboration is a professional relationship that has several distinctive components. Defining basic terms often associated with collaboration, and sometimes mistaken for collaboration, will begin to bring those distinctive components into clarity.

COOPERATION is defined by the educators' version of show-and-tell. You show me what you are doing with your students and tell me about it, and I will do the same. Cooperation is a valued affect among educators and is not to be minimized in any way.

> It's so much more friendly with two.
> A. A. Milne, *Winnie-the-Pooh*, 1926

Sharing among educators is not a given; although we all share a common goal of improved student learning, we may have very different ideas about how to best work toward achieving that goal. We all know educators who are so territorial that they are reluctant to share with their colleagues. Sometimes a team of educators will cooperate with each other but keep their collective work-product from their other colleagues. Those librarians who say that they are collaborating with their fellow teachers are often cooperating with them; they will make time or room for them or display student work in the library for Open House. Because collaboration is a relationship and cooperation is on the continuum of that professional relationship scale, cooperation is an important marker along the way. Effective cooperation builds trust and respect, which are key components of collaboration.

COORDINATION is planned cooperation. What starts out in the parking lot or the teachers' lounge as cooperative sharing might develop into a coordinated effort of meeting in the lounge every Thursday after school.

Coordinated efforts might draw in others who might not have cooperated previously. A common short-term goal of an upcoming event might spur coordinated efforts that might take hold, and a new openness to cooperation and coordination

> A told B, and B told C, "I'll meet you at the top of the coconut tree."
> Bill Martin, Jr. and John Archambault, *Chicka Chicka Boom Boom*, 1989

might actually become embedded in the school culture. Changes in school culture are generally small, incremental, repeated actions over time that allow educators to develop new habits to match those changes that they value. Administrators take notice of their professional educators demonstrating intellectual behaviors that have an impact on the culture. School climates change when those administrators understand the value of supporting embedded professional development. Savvy administrators are often able to neutralize negative forces within the school culture by being reflective educational leaders, who might offer assistance with coordinating efforts within their faculty. Highly savvy administrators know when to offer assistance and then step aside and let their educators act as the professionals that they know themselves to be.

COLLABORATION is a purposive professional relationship that develops when two or more educators bring their unique perspectives together to create something new, something beyond the capacity of any of the parties. There is a healthy desire to demonstrate trust and respect, not just for each other but for the students they are serving. Each collaborative partner has a singular vision that grows when joined in a shared vision. There is a generative aspect to collaboration that many creative collaborative partners claim by being unable to identify the genesis of an idea or the time at which another idea took over.

> It's as large as life, and twice as natural!
> Lewis Carroll, *Through the Looking-Glass*, 1871

"True collaboration" has potential to build into something explosive and beyond control, and oftentimes therein lies the rub. This creative phenomenon is written about in such lofty and grandiose terms that it scares us away from venturing forth. Comfort in cooperation is a positive step in schools, but it is not to be confused with collaboration.

Collaborative relationships take time to develop, as all relationships do. Trust between educators takes time to grow, and respect for colleagues is earned over time because it is based in personal experience. It is rare to expect that someone new to a school will begin to collaborate with others before learning the idiosyncrasies of the school learning community, the faculty, the administration, the parents, and the community. Communication channels are unique from school to school, and learning the best methods for communicating with each group of stakeholders within the school learning community is of critical importance. However, there are steps that we take to prepare ourselves so that when opportunities arise we are ready for them; we do our collaboration homework. We are comfortable discussing the *AASL Standards for 21st-Century Learners* with our colleagues; we are familiar with our curriculum structure; we prepare for classes by reviewing their instructional materials; we develop our collections to support the school curriculum and changing community demographics; we support action research; we network with other librarians; we look ahead to major events in our community; we offer to help our teachers develop their own information literacy skills; and we develop reporting relationships with our administrators that are firmly based in student learning.

> The quality of our relationships is the key to establishing a positive ethos for change. Long-lived and productive relationships spring up from a soil rich in covenants and trust.
>
> Max DePree, *Leadership Jazz*, 1993

Collaborative planning and co-teaching are key components of educator (sometimes called instructional) collaboration. In fact, it is in the planning stage that most of the creative and generative aspects of collaboration come to life. Meeting to plan collaboratively is tricky for those educators with fixed schedules, no available time during the day, and busy personal lives that preclude meeting before and after school. The reality is that planning does take front-loaded time but that the co-teaching or collaborative teaching that follows saves time by covering standards and content overlays. Virtual collaborative planning is facilitated by collaborative planning templates available on the library Web site.

Once the collaborative planning is initiated, the implementation usually includes co-teaching. Co-teaching might mean that a teacher and librarian are guiding student learning together, physically, in the same learning environment. More likely, there are instances of the teacher teaching in the classroom, the library media specialist teaching in the library, and virtual guidance is provided beyond the school day through the library and classroom Web presence. We may feel that it would be ideal for both to be present at all times, but that is not common and should not be considered a necessary element. It serves our students well to guide their learning in partnership. Of course, the teacher in the library and the librarian in the classroom are welcome experiences when possible.

It bears reiteration that the focus on instructional collaboration, with a short-term goal of integrated instruction, is in response to the understanding that information skills are best learned and retained when implemented in context. Similarly, inquiry-based learning is an effective approach to exploring most content areas, and students are served best when information literacy skills are embedded in a wide variety of learning experiences. The more authentic and engaging the learning opportunities, the more likely the transfer of skills will result, as students find enhanced personal meaning through purposeful information-seeking behaviors.

Instructional collaboration includes collaboration not only with the classroom teacher but also with the student and student groups. Authentic learning affords us rich opportunities to collaborate with our public librarians, local museum educational staff, community social service agencies, and other schools in the community.

School library practitioners are not the sole heirs to collaboration as both a mandate and a challenge. Collaboration appears in teacher and administrator standards and evalua-

> Nothing new that is really interesting comes without collaboration.
>
> James Watson, American molecular biologist and co-discoverer of the double helix (DNA), for which he won the 1962 Nobel Prize in Physiology

tion measures. Visual and performing arts teachers strive toward integrating their curriculum in the general curriculum. Creative foreign language and physical education teachers look toward collaboration for particular units of study. Special education preservice teachers are as profoundly influenced to collaborate as preservice teacher librarians. In all cases, our students suffer from unequal access to the general curriculum without collaborative efforts from our colleagues. School librarians may find kindred spirits amongst the "specials" or the other resource faculty in the school. Collaborative partnerships build, grow, wither, begin anew, as other relationships might. We learn from each experience—we learn about playing well with others, but, equally important, we learn about ourselves as both educators and learners.

The volumes of articles and books devoted to the phenomenon of collaboration are testimony to its value within the educational community. And yet, relationships are risky, and collaboration is no different. There are exposed feelings, unexpected strengths, and challenges to our pride. There are times when leadership means stepping back so that others might lead or stepping up when we would rather not. There is a vulnerability that we do not need to acknowledge when we stay safely within the confines of our minimal expectations of getting through the day. The truth is that all collaborative relationships do not succeed, despite best efforts. But, ultimately, collaboration is not about us, it is about our students.

We need to power through the rough patches, brush ourselves off, and move forward. Reflective practitioners might disagree and respond that, although it is not about us, strengthening our collaborative skills does, in fact, serve our students better. Toward that end, we do need to focus on our communication skills, sharing our vision, developing trust and respect for our colleagues, our students, and ourselves.

> Success comes from taking the path of maximum advantage instead of the path of least resistance.
>
> George Bernard Shaw, Irish playwright, 1856–1950

QUESTIONS AND ANSWERS ABOUT COLLABORATION

1. I feel very comfortable with the level of "cooperation" (which I used to call "collaboration") I have with my teachers in my building. So why leave my comfort zone and rock the boat when it might be risky?

Maybe one way to look at it is to compare your role as a professional educator with a health professional. You have an ailment that requires attention. You go to your usual health care provider. You expect that you will receive the best care possible, based on the latest research. You expect that your health care professional will take into account your age, medical history, and other pertinent data. Can you imagine if providers learned of a new intervention but chose not to incorporate it into their practice because they were comfortable with the status quo? Or treated all their patients equally regardless of mitigating factors? Collaboration serves students learning more effectively, both from a content perspective and an information literacy skills perspective. It allows for greater differentiation of instruction for students, based on firm knowledge of student abilities (teacher knowledge) and a comprehensive knowledge of authoritative resources available in all media formats (librarian knowledge). Our students are facing a future in which their information skill sets will be tested in both their academic and personal lives. We are service professionals; whether it be in health or education, we have a responsibility—our role is to best serve our community using all the means available to us.

2. I am new to my building. How do I start to collaborate if collaboration takes trust and respect and those components take time to develop? Honestly, I was in my last building for years and just never knew how to start. It felt too overwhelming. And my principal did not seem to care.

Agreed. It does sound overwhelming when you think about all your teachers, all your students, and everything else that you have to accomplish on any given day. Conventional wisdom advises you to start small and start friendly. Start with one lesson plan that has been successful for you. Start with an area that has good current coverage in your collection both in print and databases. Start with a teacher with whom you have a friendly collegial relationship. Don't worry about collaborating with every teacher every year on every unit. Stay focused on one pilot lesson plan. After the initial experience, plan to debrief together. Adjust the lesson plan as soon as the assignment is over, so that both of you will remember what needs adjusting. Start a curriculum map for yourself, where you indicate the collaborative lessons. Stake out reasonable goals, so that you move forward with all deliberate speed. From your very first experience, report student learning based on integrated instruction (including student work if possible) to appropriate administrators in a systematic communication style, whether through meetings, reports, or e-newsletters. Sometimes we find ourselves in an educational role with our administrators as well. They do not tend to have instruction in effective school library media programs, and it is our role to keep them informed about our role as an educational leader in the school Remember that your administrators are also evaluated and that collaboration is one of their benchmarks as well. Help them make the connection between the library media program and student learning.

READ MORE ABOUT COLLABORATION

American Association of School Librarians. (2008, February 29). *Collaboration.* http://www.ala.org/ala/aasl/aaslproftools/resourceguides/collaboration.cfm.
    Resource Guide posted by AASL is a one-stop shopping for a solid foundation in collaboration, both within the school and with community stakeholders. For a compilation of "best of" articles, see *Collaboration: Best of Knowledge Quest,* a 2007 AASL publication of articles previously published in *Knowledge Quest* and edited by Patricia Monteil-Overall and Donald C. Adcock. The link to Collaborative Program Planning and Teaching (provided by *Teacher Librarian*) offers a free workbook guide for the school librarian to write notes, teaching strategies, evaluation, and a checklist. Make this the first step in learning more about collaboration.

Bush, G. 2003. Do your collaboration homework. *Teacher Librarian 31*(1): 15–18.

Article focuses on a practical approach toward collaboration that favors the prepared mind. "Homework" refers to specific recommended steps for the school librarian to take that ensure effective collaborative relationships with teachers and administrators.

Bush, G. 2003. *The school buddy system: The practice of collaboration.* Chicago: American Library Association.

A framework for educator collaboration based on research is described, along with discussion prompts and thought-provoking quotes from education scholars and practitioners. Historical context for collaboration and educational theories for establishing a collaborative mind-set help define the current school climate toward collaboration.

Doll, C. A. 2005. *Collaboration and the school library media specialist.* Lanham, MD: Scarecrow Press.

Starting with the evolving national standards and indicating the necessity for collaboration in today's school library media program, Doll writes in clear terms about the theory and the practice of collaboration. Techniques for collaborative planning and instruction help the reader understand what successful collaboration looks like in the school library.

Farmer, L. S. J. 2007. *Collaborating with administrators and educational support staff: Best practices for school library media professionals.* New York: Neal-Schuman.

A guiding text for school librarians, Farmer's book provides a wealth of information regarding specific collaborative relationships with various stakeholders. Specific benefits are discussed for collaborating with teachers, reading and special education specialists, administrators, counselors, etc.

Schrage, M. 1995. *No more teams! Mastering the dynamics of creative collaboration.* NY: Doubleday.

Originally published by Random House in 1990 as *Shared Minds,* Schrage's approach to the phenomenon of collaboration underscores the empowering aspect of this human relationship. The author feels that the concept of *team* blurs our understanding; that we need to refocus our attention on the relationships within organizations. The text and User's Guide are designed for corporate organizations but could be understood within our context of the school library.

CONNECT COLLABORATION TO 21ST-CENTURY LEARNERS

The flexible learning environment of the school library lends itself not only to students working collaboratively in groups but also to students engaged in individual student projects. Savvy school librarians encourage students, even when working independently, to share resources with classmates when it might benefit others; students appreciate that level of respect for their information-seeking skills. Educators understand that when students are put in positions of sharing knowledge, it helps them interact more fully with the information they are gathering. Students also share strategies, thinking styles, and critical thinking skills when explaining which resource they are recommending, how they used it, and what justifies using that resource over others. Sharing knowledge and participating as valued members of the learning community is all about social learning and performing as valued members of a collaborative team (3.2.1, 3.2.2, 3.2.3).

School librarians who feel that students are not using the library in particularly collaborative ways for research should look to the library as a welcoming home for students pursuing personal growth. Think fun, hobbies, special-interest magazines, celebrating events, and local activities. What could you do in your library to encourage students who choose to pursue interests, share motivation, discuss interests, and enjoy literary genres together (4.2.1, 4.2.2, 4.2.3, 4.2.4)? Think about simple gatherings that give students opportunities to feel confidence in sharing and highlighting personal interests, and you might just find collaborative juices flowing that seep into cooperative learning experiences.

DISPOSITIONAL PROMPTS ABOUT COLLABORATION

1. The teachers in my school seem to be colleagues in name only. They get along very well but respect each other's space, even within their own departments. On occasion, we have had building- or district-enforced collaboration as a part of some poorly designed professional development scheme that fell flat. It seems so far out of our school culture to collaborate. Isn't it important to have professional dispositions that match those of the other educators in the building? What do we do when our field supports instructional collaboration but our administrators and teachers do not support it? P.S. We do not have any nationally board-certified teachers in our building, in case that matters.

2. In order to integrate instruction, I keep a curriculum map that I am continually updating. It is informal, but I have found that the teachers do not change their curriculum much year to year. So the students in my building are benefiting from integrated instruction, but basically I am doing it on my own. Even calling it "cooperation" would be overstating it. In fact, I think that some teachers resent that I know when a particular unit will be starting. I let them know what new resources we have available to them, but that information is not always well received. I believe that I am serving the students well. Isn't that the essence of the collaborative disposition? Does it really matter that the teachers are not a part of this equation?

A True Act of Service

Chapter Eleven

Resiliency

The primary role of school librarians is to increase student achievement. However, this becomes especially challenging when students struggle with significant family and community issues that make true academic and social engagement difficult to achieve. The number of issues facing students—such as divorce, mental illness, poverty, lack of resources and support, trauma, depression, and disability—is mind-boggling. It is not uncommon for educators to fault students for their lack of motivation and failure to achieve, even though the real problem is that the educators are unprepared to deal with the enormity and complexity of student problems and issues. The seemingly small act of getting out of bed in the morning and making it to school is a major accomplishment to a child who is bogged down with challenges that most of us cannot fathom. Even students who seem to live a charmed life need strengthening. It is a dangerous world, and the amount of random crime, tragedy, and violence, as well as economic uncertainty, is cause enough to try to bolster students. To have a true impact on students, school librarians need to understand the concept of resiliency and how people overcome life challenges.

REGGIE

Abir started out slowly. He missed a lot of school early on. When he did come to school, he filled the paper in the copier and the printers. Then he started coming at the end of the day too, and he would look at each computer and clear the desktop, check the history, just make sure they were okay before he logged them off and shut them down for the day. Still, he was very quiet and became more reserved the more I tried to talk to him. I decided to back off and just wait for him to open up to me.

It turns out that he is from a war-torn area of the world where he has never experienced peace. He has lost family members and moved around a lot. The family he is living with is related to close family friends from home. His family was worried about him when his older brother started becoming more militant, and they wanted to send Abir someplace safe and out of harm's way, at least for a while. Abir did not have a say in that decision, and he is angry with his family, and he misses them deeply at the same time. Basically, he is living with strangers, who are very kind to him, but they are pretty old and don't know how to have a pre-teen hanging around their apartment.

Abir does appear to be healthier and even growing a little bit. I see him talking to classmates once in a while. He likes to kick around the soccer ball that I keep in the back. And then, all of a sudden, he will look so sad. Last week, I told him that I wanted to have a meeting with him. I think that it scared him, which is so stupid of me. I told him not to be worried, it was a good thing, that I needed his help.

I told Abir about my idea for the tech club at our school and the district. At first, he was not pleased, which surprised me. I realized that he thought it would mean that something that was special just for him would have to be shared with others. I assured him that his job was secure and that this would be something different. We would meet once a week at lunch or something like that. I explained that I had asked to meet with him because I wanted his ideas about how to plan for the club; he was my expert because of his experience over this year. And if we had a good year with the club next year, maybe the high school would consider establishing a tech club just in time for Abir when he would be a freshman. I am going to put in some clinical hours for my grad program at the high school this summer, and I will talk about it with Patrick, the high school librarian, just to see what he thinks.

I don't know. Do you talk about plans with a student who might not be here in a few years? It is still puzzling to me that the AP thought that I would be a good connection for Abir when he first came to JHS. I wonder who she was trying to help more, him or me.

LET'S DISCUSS RESILIENCY

In the 1950s, two women—Emmy Werner, a psychologist and faculty member at the University of California at Davis, and Ruth Smith, a practicing psychologist in Hawaii, began a 40-year longitudinal study to monitor the impact of risk factors, stressful life events, and protective factors on the development of 505 children born on the island of Kauai, Hawaii in 1955 (Werner and Smith 1992). The Kauai Longitudinal Study followed the lives of these individuals through infancy, early and middle childhood, late adolescence, and adulthood. Most children in the study were born without complications, grew up in supportive environments, and coped successfully with the developmental tasks of childhood and adolescence;

however, 1 child in 3 was considered high-risk because of prenatal complications, chronic poverty, a disorganized family environment, or parents who lacked adequate education. Nevertheless, one-third of these high-risk children grew to become resilient—"competent, confident, and caring" young adults by age 18. The importance of Werner and Smith's research to school librarians is the insight it provides us about the differences between resilient overcomers and struggling high-risk youth, which may be as simple as a caring teacher. When we understand these differences, we can create school library environments, programs, services, and collections that are likely to contribute to a student's resiliency.

Werner and Smith found three clusters of protective factors that distinguish resilient overcomers from the high-risk youth who developed serious problems in childhood and adolescence. First, resilient youth had at least average intelligence and the pleasing dispositions of "robustness, vigor, and an active sociable temperament" that are used to elicit the support of family members, teachers, friends, and even strangers, who mentored, nurtured, and helped them succeed (192). Second, resilient youth benefited from grandparents and older siblings, who acted as parent substitutes to encourage trust, autonomy, and initiative. Third, resilient youth had an external support system in church, youth groups, and school that—in army lingo, helped them "be all you can be" and provided a soft place to land when difficulties arose.

> I can see how teachers would be a little weary of an "at risk" student. But it doesn't necessarily mean that we're dumb or that "at risk" [students] are less able to do things, it just means that sometimes for circumstances beyond their control they're "at risk."
>
> L. W. S., high school student

In addition, Werner and Smith (1992) found that resilient children had the following behaviors:

- They set goals for themselves, and "nowhere were the differences between the resilient individuals and their peers with problems in adolescence more apparent than in the goals they had set themselves for their adult lives"(69).
- They considered "their personal competence and determination to be their most effective resource in dealing with stressful life events" (70).
- They were critical thinkers and problem solvers, and "more often than not they took their own counsel when it came to major decisions in their lives" (68).
- They were competent readers by grade four and "had significantly higher scores on the STEP Reaching achievement test than did their high risk peers who developed coping problems in adulthood" (176).
- They benefited from nurturing adults, and "a caring teacher was an important protective factor for boys and girls who succeeded against the odds" (178).

It is possible to apply Werner and Smith's resiliency research to the school library, because protective factors that tip the balance from high-risk to resilient are—or should be—central functions of the school library. The "64-thousand dollar question" becomes "How do school librarians apply the concept of resiliency to strengthen youth?"

Two frameworks are helpful for school librarians who want to promote resilience in students. The first framework is the *Resiliency Wheel* created by Nan Henderson, the founder of

Resiliency in Action at www.resiliency.com. Youth are strengthened in two ways. The first is to *strengthen* the environment in the following ways:

- Provide care and support, so students feel they matter.
- Set high expectations, so students feel worthy and confident about their place in the school and world and will rise up to meet expectations.
- Provide opportunities for students to develop their talents and abilities and participate in the life of the school.

Likewise, the second way youth are strengthened is to *diminish* risk factors in the environment in the following ways:

- Encourage pro-social bonding to ensure that every student has someone in the school to depend on.
- Set fair, clear, and consistent boundaries and rules, so students are treated fairly and "buy in" to boundaries and rules.
- Teach students a variety of life skills, such as assertiveness, problem solving, stress management, and healthy conflict resolution, so students can successfully negotiate their environments.

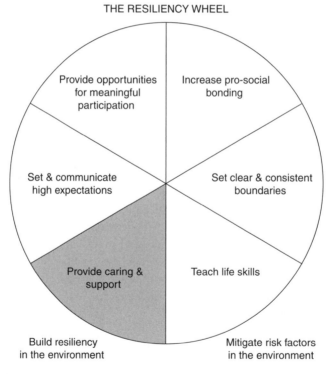

Figure 11.1   The Resiliency Wheel

Source: Nan Henderson and Resiliency in Action at www.resiliency.com. Reprinted by permission.

A second framework for strengthening youth is the *Library Ladder of Resiliency,* which consists of five rungs, each representing a protective factor found in Werner and Smith's resiliency research. The five rungs are mentoring, reading, problem solving, social skills, and hobbies and interests. Although the five rungs are likely being carried out, school librarians who realize the power and importance of these seemingly minor actions to build resilience are apt to become more intentional about using them.

The first rung of The Library Ladder of Resiliency is mentoring, which is perhaps the single most important resiliency-promoting strategy of all. The definition of mentoring is to provide guidance, support, reassurance, friendship, and perspective to a young person. It is surprising how many educators are mean to students and treat them disrespectfully, which only fuels a downward spiral. Many students will not engage in academics unless they are cared for and respected. According to the research and writings on Millennials, a generation of youth born about 1980, respect is required before true engagement ever occurs. Millennials respond to coaxing and encouragement, not harsh directives or commands. Knowing a student's name and his or her passions and goals is the starting point to developing a nurturing and accepting environment that appeals to youth.

> Resilience research makes clear that protective factors in one setting have the power to compensate for risks that may be present in other settings.
>
> Bonnie Benard, resiliency expert

The second rung is reading. Norman Garmazy's (1983) research on poor black youth in London found that children who exhibited qualities of resilience lived in homes "marked by the presence of books" (75). Struggling youth are able to use words, stories, and books to transport themselves to places that are softer, warmer, and more accepting than real life. Research shows that stories and books help struggling high-risk youth, especially boys, imagine "what if."

The third rung is problem solving and life skills. Sometimes struggling youth compound their problems because they do not possess the necessary skills to negotiate life as their more resilient and competent peers do.

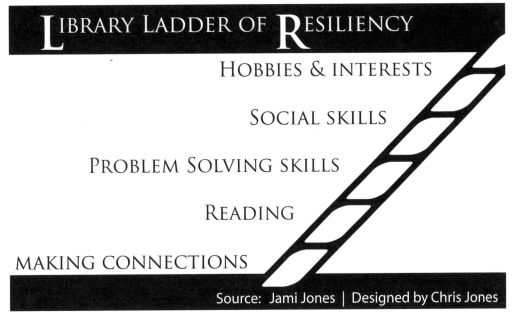

Figure 11.2   The Library Ladder of Resiliency

Source: Reprinted by permission of the author.

The fourth rung is social skills. Youth who have well-developed social skills make and keep friends who will hang with them during trying times. Like dispositions, social skills are taught by fostering, encouraging, and modeling these behaviors. School

> I thought I could. I thought I could. I thought I could. I thought I could. I thought I could. I thought I could.
> Watty Piper, *The Little Engine that Could*, 1930

librarians promote social skills when they support and host activities that encourage students to make connections and work with each other.

The fifth rung is hobbies and interests that provide a natural opportunity to socialize and make friends with others who are interested in the same activities. They learn that "practice makes perfect" and with patience and effort all things are possible.

School librarians who embrace resiliency will likely build school libraries similar to Nelle Martin's. Nelle, a school librarian at a Catholic school in West Palm Beach, Florida, noticed each day that the same students sat alone to the school library during lunch rather than eat with friends in the cafeteria. Curiosity and concern drove her to talk to these students, and she found that most were new to the school and had not made friends. Nelle introduced these students to one another, to form a group called the *Lunch Bunch,* bought board games to play during lunch, and let them eat in a corner of the school library. Nelle was truly amazed to see these students flourish. Other than spending a little money and easing up on rules, the core of

> Like parenting, teaching is a mission, not just a task or a job.
> Marian Wright Edelman, activist and founder of the Children's Defense Fund

this program, which dramatically changed the high school experience for a dozen students, consists of two dispositions—empathy and concern. Nelle Martin's *Lunch Bunch* program stands as a model for all of us who want to create a place where students can reach their full potential.

REFERENCES

Garmazy, N. 1983. Stressors of childhood. In *Stress, coping, and development in children,* eds. Norman Garmazy and Michael Rutter, 43–84. New York: McGraw-Hill.

Henderson, N., and M. M. Milstein. 2003. *Resiliency in schools: Making it happen for students and educators.* Thousand Oaks, CA: Corwin Press.

Werner, E. E., and R. S. Smith. 1992. *Overcoming the odds: High risk children from birth to adulthood.* Ithaca, NY: Cornell University.

QUESTIONS AND ANSWERS ABOUT RESILIENCY

1. All this sounds great, but at my school all that matters is end-of-grade test scores and annual yearly progress. I still need more persuading. How will an emphasis on resiliency help raise test scores?

    I can understand your wariness; this is a different approach for many school librarians who teach in schools that emphasize the cognitive domain at the expense of the affective side of students. Let me give you one example. Stress is a major cause of depression. Although each of us experiences stress, how we handle it is what matters. Some of us are able to structure our time and understand the importance of healthy living and adequate sleep in mitigating the effects of stress. When students successfully handle stress and are able to concentrate on academics, end-of-grade test scores will be higher than if we had left them to muddle in their problems and cope by themselves. It is just good common sense to realize that students who are stressed and close to the breaking point cannot focus on academics. Strengthening the whole child leads to higher test scores.

2. The guidance counselor at my school is very powerful, and she tells me that I should not be concerned with student's self-esteem because that is her job, not mine. She says I should be content with checking out books. I do not agree, but what can I do?

The care and nurturing of students is *everyone's* concern and responsibility. The research clearly shows what helps build student resilience. You come into contact with students daily and are well positioned to mentor and nurture, encourage pro-social bonding, set boundaries, provide opportunities for meaningful participation, and teach life skills.

No matter how much power this guidance counselor has, her understanding of the role of the school librarian is limited, as well as her recognition that it "takes a village to raise a child." Perhaps, because she has never observed a proactive and collaborative school librarian, it will be up to you to communicate the importance of the school library to the academic achievement and affective development of students. Your first step is to raise the school library's visibility by informing all constituent groups—teachers, administrators, students, and parents—that resiliency principles are the foundation of programs and services. Second, initiate meetings with various departments and groups throughout the school to begin the conversation about resiliency and ways to strengthen youth. Make sure you do your homework before you go to these meetings, so you can suggest changes rather than ask "What can I do for you?" Third, plan collaboratively with teachers who are most open to working with you. Read Chapter Ten on collaboration to learn more. Just as school librarians must collaborate, so must guidance counselors.

READ MORE ABOUT RESILIENCY

Doll, B., S. Zucker, and K. Brehm. 2004. *Resilient classrooms: Creating healthy environments for learning.* New York: Guildford Press.

The authors have written a practical book, grounded in cutting-edge theory and research, to help all educators to create caring and nurturing learning environments. The book contains easy-to-apply tools and classroom-based strategies for promoting the academic achievement and emotional well-being of students.

Henderson, N., B. Benard, and N. Sharp-Light. 2007. *Resiliency in action: Practical ideas for overcoming risks and building strengths in youth, families, and communities.* Ojai, CA: Resiliency in Action.

Along with strategies and valuable information to move your family, school, community, children, and youth from risk to resiliency, this book provides research findings, interviews and advice, and stories of youth who have bounced back from gang and drug involvement, pregnancy, and academic failure.

Humphrey, M. 2008. *Bounce back!: Resiliency strategies through children's literature*. Westport, CT: Libraries Unlimited.

Humphrey illustrates the power of resiliency through 20 lesson plans that center on using a picture or chapter book to bounce back from life's challenges and adversity. Each lesson provides an introduction to the story, a list of characters, a tool box chart of resiliency skills, discussion questions, classroom activities, and book reviews.

Jones, J. L. 2007. *Bouncing back: Dealing with the stuff life throws at you*. New York: Franklin Watts.

Jones has written a book accessible to middle school-aged children, based on the Werner and Smith's Kauai Longitudinal Study, to help youth to bounce back from stress and challenges. *Bouncing Back* provides practical strategies for adolescents who are dealing with life's hard knocks, as well as the caring adults who act as supports.

CONNECT RESILIENCY TO 21ST-CENTURY LEARNERS

In the book *Resiliency in School: Making it Happen for Students and Educators,* Nan Henderson and Mike M. Milstein (2003) describe the characteristics of resilient students. Resilient students exhibit these traits:

- Believe their voice is heard in classroom and with school decisions
- Participate in helping others
- Believe that any goal or aspiration can be achieved
- Show confidence in self and others
- Feel that the school is a caring place
- Have a sense of belonging
- Connect with at least one of the many caring adults in the school
- Are positively connected to learning
- Are involved with before-, after-, and in-school activities
- Understand and abide by policies and rules
- Participate in changing rules
- Receive ongoing instruction in life skills
- Integrate and practice life skills (30)

A school librarian who strengthens the environment by setting and communicating high expectations creates students who believe that goals or aspirations can be accomplished, show confidence in themselves and others, and encourage themselves and others to be their best. These resilient students meet AASL Dispositions in Action 1.2.6, to "display emotional resilience by persisting in information searching despite challenges," and 2.2.4, to "demonstrate personal productivity by completing products to express learning." School librarians diminish risk factors in the environment by increasing pro-social bonding, so students connect with at least one caring adult in the school, are involved with school activities, are engaged in cooperative peer-to-peer interactions, and are positively connected to learning. These resilient students meet AASL Dispositions in Action 3.2.2, to "show social responsibility by participating actively with others in learning situations and by contributing questions and ideas during group discussions." For each spoke of the Resiliency Wheel, it is possible to match the characteristics of resilient students to dispositions identified in the AASL *Standards for the 21st-Century Learner.*

DISPOSITIONAL PROMPTS ABOUT RESILIENCY

1. Many students at my school lead complex and chaotic lives. I hear about these students and worry about their future, but I do not know how to help. Just the other day, I found a student, who was supposed to be in class, crying at one of the tables because her parents are divorcing. A student who is not in class is supposed to be written up and given detention. In this case, detention seems harsh to me. I do not feel that I am in a position right now to change school policy, but I want to be sensitive to students. Books or courses in our field focus on collection development or reference, not on these softer skills that I think I need to work with today's high-risk and struggling students. If we embrace the concept of resiliency and strive to build a school library that strengthens students, what does this look like? What should I be doing?

2. I have made changes this year to my school library to improve the way it is viewed by students. A few have commented about how much "happier" it seems to them. First, I am putting into place *The Library Ladder of Resiliency.* Second, I have had students help me modify the school library's rules to make them less rigid. I agree with these changes. Third, I learned every student's name and, whenever possible, greet them by name as they enter and leave the school library. In my district, what I am doing is out of step with other school librarians, who are not so considerate of students and emphasize instruction over the affective needs of students. Is it alright for me to be a "lone ranger," or should I try to influence my school librarian colleagues about the importance of resiliency?

Chapter Twelve

Leadership

Your school library might have the fastest computers in the district. It might even have adopted a flexible schedule. Perhaps you spent last year creating a curriculum map. Even with all these positives, the school library may not be making a difference. As much as you repeat the mantra, "the school library is the heart of the school," your message seems to fall on deaf ears. You feel you are not taken seriously as an instructional leader, and you are exhausted at the thought of fighting for your budget yet another year. What do you do?

LISA

It was a good year overall. But it is funny how the bad things stick out in our memories. I really fouled up with that one idea about the teachers' reading club. I decided to talk to Dr. Kelly about it, even though the mantra in our school is not to seek out her advice unless it is really just to get a gold star from the principal.

So I made an appointment with her after school on a beautiful spring day. We sat on a bench in the courtyard. She said, "It's your nickel," which I know means that her time is short and I should get to the point. It is hard for me to tell her that I think I have a problem communicating. Imagine that. So I stay specific to that one conversation, one idea, and ask for her advice. She says that the teachers might not have been reacting to the idea as much as the timing. We were discussing new methods of assessment at that faculty meeting, and the teachers were upset about it. And it was the holidays. And I was suggesting something completely out of the blue that would be something else on their plates. Dr. Kelly said that she felt sorry for me at the time but that I need to learn how you get people to want to agree with you. I do feel like she likes me (doesn't dislike me?) or at least that she sees potential in me. I know that I have a lot to learn, and I am just trying to figure how to learn it.

Dr. Kelly recommended that I look for some summer professional development that focuses on children's literature. While I am there, I should network and maybe develop the kind of reading group I was trying to form at WES. Or maybe work with the PTO leadership and create a parent and grandparent reading group for children's books. I had never thought of it that way. Everything she suggested made sense and sounded interesting but drawn out and slow to me.

Dr. Kelly told me that growing as a professional has setbacks and that I have to understand that wanting to develop my skills is a quality of a true leader. Those setbacks come with the territory (she said *especially* in an elementary school) and that we "solos" have to stick together. I was so surprised by this whole conversation. I do realize that, on any given day, I might have had a different response from Dr. Kelly. But on this spring day, without a cloud in the sky, I felt like my principal was heading me on a new path. She smiles at me, and I start to feel like my eyes were glazing over. Maybe I am not who she sees in me, as I start to think about just dropping the whole idea and going for a walk when I get home. I might have to withstand her disappointment in me, but that will be alright; I know myself enough to know that it is better than starting on a path I have no intention of following.

LET'S DISCUSS LEADERSHIP

The key to becoming the most important place in the school is your leadership. Simply put, leadership is influence. You cannot move the school library program from "good enough" to "heart of the school" without possessing the disposition of leadership to make this happen. Think of Point A as the starting point—you are *telling* members of the school community that the school library is the heart of the school. Point B is the realization by students, teachers, and administrators that it *is* the heart of the school. It is your leadership ability that moves the library from Point A to Point B. When school librarians complain about being ignored and not supported, it is a good bet that a lack of leadership skills is the culprit. School librarians wanting to build an exemplary school library program must focus on the power of leadership.

There are two ways to become an effective leader. The first way is to work harder, but this may not get you the desired results because you can only work so hard. There are only so many hours in a day. Besides, at some point the Law of Diminishing Returns kicks in. Although this is an economic concept, it has implications for us. What this law states is that more and more input (work) eventually leads to less and less output (results). In addition, not all activities reap the same benefit. For instance, shelving books (although important) does not leverage your program the same way that becoming an instructional leader does. It is important to focus on those activities that will bring you closer to your final destination, which is Point B—the heart of the school. The second way to succeed is by becoming a successful leader disposed to leadership, which is our focus.

It is important to realize two things about leadership. First, put out of your head the nonsense that some people are natural born leaders whereas others are not. Although it is true that some people are naturally talented in this area, it is equally true that, if you are willing to do what it takes to become a better leader, you will succeed. Second, leadership is not about making more money or becoming a principal or bossing others around because you have the power to do so—leadership is about influence.

For the school library to become the heart of the school rather than a mere slogan, school librarians must influence members of the school community to understand the power of an effective school library program to raise academic achievement and strengthen students. The primary reason for school librarians to become leaders is not to receive accolades, but to benefit students and teachers alike. To ask others to support the school library program, collaborate, and implement information literacy requires that the school librarian exhibit the following leadership qualities:

1. *Character.* Pure and simple, leadership is influence; however, several factors come into play. The most important factor is character, which consists of a group of attributes, such as ethics, trustworthiness, honesty, and good work habits. School librarians with strong character care for members of the school community and want what is best for them. They put people first and recognize that the purpose of the school library is to empower teachers to teach more effectively and to strengthen students academically, emotionally, and socially, not simply to further the program.

2. *Learning.* Leadership is a learning process. You *learn* to be a leader by observing leaders you respect and by reading on the topic. Read about leaders. Go to workshops. Sign up for leadership initiatives. Furthermore, learning about leadership is a lifelong commitment.

> Leadership is a potent combination of strategy and character. But if you must be without one, be without strategy.
> Norman Schwarzkopf,
> U.S. Army General (ret.)

3. *Touching the heart.* When it comes to working with people, the heart comes before the head. You cannot influence and move people to action unless you first move them with emotion. In order to do this, the school librarian must work diligently to connect with teachers, staff, administrators, and students. Take a moment to connect relationally before you get down to the nitty gritty of work. The stronger the connection, the more likely you will garner support in your quest to make the school library the heart of the school. A leader does not have to be listed in the top tier of the organizational chart to be effective—leadership is not dependent on position, and it is not a fancy title. Position alone does not ascribe leadership or influence. The term *positional leadership* describes people who have the title but may or may not have the influence. Margaret Thatcher, the former British prime minister, once said, "Being in power is like being a lady. If you have to tell people you are, you aren't" (Maxwell 2007, 16). A school librarian who is (or is becoming) a bona fide leader will find ways to communicate to colleagues that he or she supports their success through instructional partnerships and collaborations. To connect with others, the following actions are important:
   - Articulate what it means for the school library to be the heart of the school. See Chapter Eight on communication. Write down your thoughts. Practice so that you can deliver a speech about the importance of the school library on a moment's notice. Study resources so you can verbalize the importance of the school library and why collaboration, flexible scheduling, and information literacy are so important.

- Know your audience. Who is teaching which subjects? What is their teaching style? How will this individual respond to your advocacy message?
- Initiate connections and contacts with members of the school family. To do this, you must venture outside the four walls of the school library and mix with teachers and administrators.
- Live your message. Dispositions must be modeled. As the school librarian, rely on information to make decisions. Know the courses teachers are teaching and what is going on in the classroom. Be proactive and step in to suggest resources for a lesson or a collaboration. Go the extra mile even when it is not expected.
- Do not whine. Sometimes decisions are made that have a negative impact on the school library, and we end up without the necessary resources to run the type of first-rate program we know we could if conditions were better. Other times we find ourselves wrangling with our colleagues, who are trying to run their own first-rate programs with the same limited resources we are all vying for. Flexible scheduling is one example. Flexible scheduling is valued in our profession as the preferred type of schedule, but it does require additional human resources, such as a library assistant to check out books and to "hold down the fort" as we are out and about collaborating and teaching. It is easy to become negative when our requests for a flexible schedule that *we know would help our program flourish* are ignored. Instead, resist negativity and do not whine. Follow the leadership steps in this chapter by communicating effectively, meeting with your principal to discuss your plans for the school library, and collaborating with teachers. In some little way, begin to implement small changes as *if* you had a flexible schedule. Your principal and teachers may need to see you collaborate and go the extra mile before a change in schedule is made.

4. *Good communication.* School library leaders communicate to members of the school community the value of the library and the importance of reading and information

> Great souls have wills; feeble ones have only wishes.
>
> Chinese proverb

literacy to promote life skills, curiosity, and personal development and enjoyment. School librarians may need to develop a variety of communication skills, such as public speaking, writing, Web design, and social networking. If you are weak in any of these areas, this is the time to learn.

5. *Vision.* Leaders are both highly visionary as well as practical—they experience today while focusing on tomorrow. The difference between a manager and a leader is that the former administers the here and now, but leaders are stewards of the future. Their focus is where to go and how to get there. An educational leader has a vision for a more effective school, with engaged students who use information to improve their life and work. School library leaders must communicate to administrators, faculty, and staff the purpose and goals of the school library program through finely crafted mission and vision statements that paint a picture of the library's value and potential. The plan you develop becomes the strategy for obtaining the vision and meeting the mission. Strategy is practical and based on the mission, vision, and knowledge of the school and the district, how to get things done, and the movers and shakers. However, keep in

mind that your colleagues must buy into *you* before your vision is accepted. To bring them around, set a good example. Many classroom teachers do not understand the role of the school librarian. They may be a little envious that you do not grade papers at night and can read on the job, or it could be as silly as having a restroom in the school library. Be sensitive to how you are viewed, and help teachers understand the vital role of the school library program by supporting them in various ways.

6. *Persistence.* Many educators work in bureaucratic systems in which it is difficult to instill vision and passion. Unfortunately, there are teachers and administrators who are simply marking time until retirement. An example of persistence is Jamie Escalante, a teacher

> Charlotte was naturally patient. She knew from experience that if she waited long enough, a fly would come into her web.
> E. B. White, *Charlotte's Web*, 1952

who is the subject of the movie *Stand and Deliver.* Escalante was one of the finest teachers in Bolivia before he and his family immigrated to the United States. He went back to school so he could earn the credentials to teach in the United States. At 43 years of age, he was hired at Garfield High School in East Los Angeles, California, to teach computer science. On the first day of school, he found chaos and rampant gang activity on the campus and no computers in his classroom. "Almost daily he thought of quitting. But his passion for teaching and his dedication to improving the lives of his students wouldn't allow him to give up" (Matthews 1988, 202).

Escalante did not give up. He believed that the way to improve the school was to challenge the school's best and brightest with a calculus class that would prepare them for an AP test earning them college credit. As a result of his persistence, vision, character, and influence, he was able to begin a process of momentum:

> In 1987, nine years after Escalante spearheaded the program, Garfield students took more than 325 AP examinations. Most incredibly, Garfield had a waiting list of more than four hundred students from areas outside its boundaries wanting to enroll. The school that was once the laughingstock of the district and that had almost lost its accreditation had become one of the top three inner-city school in the entire nation! (Matthews 1988, 4)

Escalante had a vision, fortitude, and conviction to stick with it. He was able to communicate this to others, who eventually followed his example by creating and teaching other AP subjects. Escalante is a leader.

7. *Priorities.* When we are busy, we naturally believe that we are achieving. But busyness does not equal productivity. Activity is not necessarily accomplishment. Develop a vision statement, objectives, and short- and long-range plans. Leaders are not born but gain influence by being disposed to leadership.

REFERENCES

Matthews, J. 1988. *Escalante: The best teacher in America.* NY: Henry Holt and Company.

Maxwell, J. 2007. *The 21 irrefutable laws of leadership: Follow them and people will follow you.* Nashville, TN: Thomas Nelson.

QUESTIONS AND ANSWERS ABOUT LEADERSHIP

1. Isn't it enough that the school library seems to run smoothly?

No, it is not good enough. Doing what is expected is just that—it is expected and satisfactory, but not remarkable. However, to build your program to be the true "heart of the school" requires much, much more. For the media program to move beyond a passable support system—to one that is truly supportive of student achievement—requires a school librarian who is able to inspire a vision about the role of information literacy. So much of what the school librarian does depends on leadership. For instance, collaboration and many of the other topics discussed in this book are dependent on the librarian being a leader, having a vision for the school library program, and communicating this vision.

2. My school library runs on a fixed schedule, but I am trying to convince teachers and the principal that a flexible schedule is best, but so far, no luck. Do you think I might be more convincing if my leadership skills were better?

Absolutely. Leadership is so fundamental to your job that you cannot think of it simply as something nice to have, but rather a requirement to do your job. As stated earlier in this chapter, leadership is influence—pure and simple. So before you can begin to hope to convince teachers and your principal that flexible access is the better schedule, they must believe and have confidence in you. Reread this chapter very carefully and consider it your guide and framework for adopting a flexible schedule. First, understand all aspects of flexible and fixed scheduling and the pros and cons of each. You must be able to articulate what flexible scheduling is, how and why it would be beneficial to students, teachers, principal, and you (note the order—do not just focus on you!). Second, establish a relationship with teachers, if you have not already, to understand their struggles. Teachers will want to understand how flexible scheduling can help them. Third, do not use the argument "This is what I would do if the library's schedule was flexible" because this may be viewed as an empty promise. A better strategy is to influence the principal to create small blocks of flexible time within the fixed schedule so collaborative instruction can occur. Be sure to keep track of how this time is used and the benefits to students and teachers. This may seem difficult, but the saying "no pain, no gain" applies here.

READ MORE ABOUT LEADERSHIP

Goleman, D., R. E. Boyatzis, and A. McKee. 2002. *Primal leadership: Learning to lead with emotional leadership*. Cambridge, MA: Harvard University Press.

Goleman, Boyatzis, and McKee coin a new term, "primal leadership"—meaning that the essence of leadership is emotional intelligence.

Kouzes, J. M., and B. Z. Posner. 2002. *The leadership challenge*. 3rd ed. NY: Jossey-Bass.

Considered a classic, Kouzes and Posner's pragmatic and humanistic book is written on the topic of leadership. There are chapters on the practices of exemplary leadership, modeling and inspiring leadership, and encouraging the heart.

Maxwell, J. 2007. *The 21 irrefutable laws of leadership: Follow them and people will follow you.* Nashville, TN: Thomas Nelson.

An easy-to-read and easy-to-understand book about leadership. The 21 short chapters correspond to 21 laws of leadership, such as the laws of influence, priorities, and timing.

CONNECTING LEADERSHIP TO 21ST-CENTURY LEARNERS

The purpose for becoming a leader is to model these dispositions for students and to further the influence and impact of the school library program. One way we do this is by cultivating student leaders. This is truly a gift we can give students. What does a student leader look like? We promote student leadership skills by meeting the AASL Dispositions in Action standards 1.2.7, to "display persistence by continuing to pursue information to gain a broad perspective," and 3.2.1, to "demonstrate leadership and confidence by presenting ideas to others in both formal and informal situations." School librarians cultivate leadership among students when they develop instruction requiring them to influence and debate others. These resilient students meet AASL Dispositions in Action standard 1.2.1, to "display initiative and engagement by posing questions and investigating the answers beyond the collection of superficial facts."

DISPOSITIONAL PROMPTS ABOUT LEADERSHIP

1. I am following a succession of school librarians who had no influence whatsoever. Several teachers have even told me that these school librarians (who *are* credentialed and have the MLS) never left the office and didn't seem to want to work with them at all. Their cumulative neglect of the school library program has left such a bad "taste," and unfortunately I am the one who is paying for their neglect, but I really want to create the type of school library identified in the Impact Study research (available at www.lrs.org/school.php). How do I begin to build influence?

2. I know I am probably one of the school librarians described in the first prompt. I didn't intend to neglect the library or sit in the office all day, but I was so overwhelmed by the different duties and the lack of support that it was easier to complain rather than do something. At some point, no one wanted to be around me because I was so negative. I know I must have a reputation that I don't do anything, because it is difficult for me to get a job. I want to change and become the type of leader discussed in this chapter. Is it too late for me, or should I move to a different district? If I stay, how do I rebuild my reputation and become a leader?

Chapter Thirteen

Professional Ethics

The person who administers the school library is often alone in this endeavor. Classroom teachers, administrators, and other educators and staff have very different roles in the life of the school. The school librarian operates the only academic service unit within the school and is challenged by daily decisions that often make that position feel even more singular. Our professional ethics, like core values, act as a compass that helps guide the school librarian along the path. We find that, while best practices in management and administration provide the science, professional ethics provide the art in our field. The solo journey is benefited by self-reflection and networking with other kindred spirits at school libraries.

DONNA

I have to say I have been nothing short of inspirational. Working with Jenn and Marta as equal partners was so rewarding. I actually allowed myself to feel professional satisfaction in the library. That sounds so silly, especially with the way that the library is viewed at LHS. But that made me realize that the way that the library is seen by others has so much to do with how I view the library and my role as the librarian in the school. I don't know if I came into school libraries from the classroom with the wrong impression and just continued to feel that way as a result of inertia, or if I really believed that the library program should be something other than what it is and I consciously have been keeping it from becoming better out of fear of the unknown and uncomfortable. Maybe I had so much going on in my personal life I needed for my work life to be stable and predictable. For whatever reason, I am seeing things differently now, and it is making me happier in my work. I loved collaborating with those few teachers. I remembered how it felt to be a teacher again; it seemed that the students rose to the occasion, and now I want to see how I could bring even more to the table as a full collaborative partner the next time I plan an interdisciplinary library lesson. But I don't want to get carried away either.

My first thought is that, even though we had a good experience collaborating, the next time I need to think about our resources. Because our student body is changing and we have more nationalities represented, maybe our collection should reflect that change. Even the books that we do have are old and just not the right books for the students I am serving. I still need to support the core curriculum with the library budget.

Maybe I will ask Jenn and Marta if they know how to write grants and want to think about writing a proposal for a district grant. Our district offers teachers mini-grants, but I have never written one. A grant proposal could build on the collaborative unit that we developed. I could look for other grant writing workshops for our teachers, and, as I find summer professional development opportunities in our area, I could post information about them on the school Web site in the Teachers' Lounge.

I do realize that, if I want to move into the teaching aspect of the library, I will need more assistance with the maintenance-level duties, which means adding support staff—either through hiring, student workers, or volunteers. Suddenly, this way of thinking about the library program is feeling big instead of small and scary instead of friendly. Take a deep breath, Dee, pick up the latest Jodi Picoult, and relax. Help the teachers feel professional, think about how good it feels to empower them, and keep everything else nice and comfortable the way it is. Summer is almost here, and there is a graduation party to plan.

LET'S DISCUSS PROFESSIONAL ETHICS

A discussion of professional ethics does not presume that all of those who work in school libraries are professionals. However, there are ethics that guide our approach to school librarianship that benefit all of us, regardless of our academic preparation or level of engagement in the school library media center. Paraprofessional aides, parent volunteers, and student workers who focus on the maintenance issues of a school library will understand more fully management and administrative decisions if professional ethics are shared with them. Although decisions seem easier to make when there are fundamental understandings that can be explained, we are constantly balancing our societal responsibility against the rights of the individual. Each type of library has individual needs, based on the population that library serves. School librarians in public schools, parochial schools, and independent schools operate on different agendas, but they each have an agenda set by their governing institutions. Talk to a librarian in almost any situation, and you will uncover universal ethics that guide their professional lives:

SERVICE

Librarianship is a service profession. While health professionals solve health needs and car mechanics help cars operate smoothly, librarians, as information professionals, help solve information needs. We serve all members of the school learning community; we serve our colleagues at other libraries and are served by them through interlibrary loan. This service orientation does not negate the importance of leadership. In fact, service leadership is a powerful stance and is very effective for many school library professionals. "What can I do to help?" is a question that is not viewed as servile, but as compassionate.

This dedication to service should not be undervalued, even in the starkest school library environment. If we are not of service to our students and learning community, there is not a library program. The room with books and the Web site with resources does not equate to a school library. The knowledgeable, approachable, competent school librarian is an integral part of the effective school library program. Students and faculty members who are treated with respect will return the favor. Determining more efficient management of time, space, personnel, and resources relates to the professional ethic of service. That which helps us serve the needs of our library users helps us fulfill our mission.

EQUITABLE ACCESS

> You don't have to burn books to destroy a culture. Just get people to stop reading them.
> Ray Bradbury, American science fiction author

Librarians believe that all individuals have a right to unfettered access to resources and that intellectual freedom is a tenet of our profession. In school libraries, we face challenges on book titles and students accessing inappropriate Web sites. We have collection development policies that describe the actions taken when a book is challenged. In many cases, parents have not read the book, have seen words or a few ideas that are disagreeable to them, and decide not only that their child should not have access to the book but that no one's child should read the book. We applaud those parents who have concerns that they want to share; we give them a good listening to, and they understand the value of the inclusion of that title in the library. The vast majority of challenges against books in the United States come from parents who are objecting to a book in the school library or curriculum. In other cases, we are the censors. There is a fine line that distinguishes selection according to the collection development policy from censorship. School librarians who practice censorship are acting on the belief that they are avoiding censorship issues from the community, when, in fact, they are doing a disservice to their students and the community.

A practice limiting equitable access to resources may be as innocuous as the current trend in labeling books with readability levels. The censorship becomes subtle because access to resources is limited based on reading levels. Reading research shows that students aspire to read at higher levels when engaged in the content; that intrinsic motivation is affected negatively when books are labeled with defining readability levels that influence book selection. The library is an independent reading environment, designed both to support the curriculum and to foster a love of reading. Obstacles to developing a passion for reading do not sit well with librarians, who are dedicated to providing a rich, engaging reading environment in which students pursue reading as budding lifelong learners. This behavior also transfers to public library usage, where students are confronted by an often larger collection without the limiting identifying labels.

READING

Librarians believe that reading is the key to the kingdom that will set you free, let you live many lives, see things you would not have seen, have

> Circumscribed as my life was in so many ways, I had to look between the covers of books for news of the world that lay outside my own.
> Helen Keller, American author, political activist and lecturer. Keller was the first deafblind person to earn a Bachelor of Arts degree, 1880–1968

adventures, make friends, feel deeply, laugh loudly, and grow, grow, grow—and additionally increase your reading comprehension, fluency, and vocabulary. Supporting the school curriculum with literature, making content area connections to resources in a variety of formats, and fostering engaged readers is fundamental to the operation of any school library. Administrators who are fortunate enough to have well-prepared professional school librarians benefit from their vision and their library media program. Those librarians tend to have rich, current library collections; healthy opportunities for collaboration with classroom teachers and public librarians; direct connections to their technology partners; relationships with parent and community groups; and a deep respect for every student and his or her ability to learn and lead a meaningful life.

PRIVACY

Librarians protect library users' privacy and confidentiality regardless of the person's age. This professional ethic is deeply rooted in codes of ethics and practice in every library environment. Privacy usually refers to the person and confidentiality to the records of library use. In public libraries, there are occasions when library records are requested by federal law enforcement, and, to protect privacy, library users' names are kept separate from the circulation record of library materials. In most instances in the school library, this professional ethic is demonstrated by what is called the "face value rule," by which we help library users but do not pry personally. We also encourage teachers to honor this. Reading is a private act, and checking out books is also private; we do not comment or criticize. Information about book check-out patterns are confidential. Our students need to know that we respect them as individuals with rights and that we will not betray confidences. After all, we work in a service-oriented field that is built upon the honor system; we trust that our materials will be returned. It is rare to find a profession more trusting and dedicated to the betterment of society, as evidenced by daily lending of our most valuable resources. We value that time-tested handshake, and our users have every right to trust us with their private information.

> No one's private rights ought to get invaded even if it's with kindness.
> Joseph Krumgold, *Onion John*, 1959

In settings where students interact with library aides, volunteers, and student helpers, this professional ethic is perhaps the most important to share with school library staff. Invasion of privacy and restricting freedom of thought should not be tolerated. Naturally, this stance supports those who may disagree with us and enjoy making that point known. Here is where we check our compass to ensure that we are staying firmly on the path.

DEMOCRACY

Librarians are proud to be the bastions that uphold the pillars of democracy. The school library is a microcosm of the library world. Students learn how to "do library" in our school libraries, and we are hopeful that those skills will transfer as our students become academic and public library users. We value ethical uses of information, including a respect for authorship in any media format. There are materials on every topic with diverse perspectives, even those that are disagreeable to us. The library is a learning center: what better place to explore various points of view and perspectives? If a student lands in a Web site that is inappropriate, we call that a teachable moment. If a student sees language that is questionable in a book, we take the opportunity to discuss the relevance of the use of language within the context of the story.

> In true democracy every man and women is taught to think for himself or herself.
> Mohandas K. Gandhi, Indian political leader, 1869–1948

The independent learning environment of the school library is an effective breeding ground for informed citizens, who are cognizant of social responsibility and the needs of others. It is a natural place for the school climate to demonstrate a belief in a better society; all students have needs; all students can be leaders; all students can learn to serve. The library organizes the world's knowledge without exceptions. The library makes available resources to further our students' understanding of that world and to help them find their place in it.

> You mean you're comparing our lives to a sonnet? A strict form, but freedom within it? Yes . . . You're given the form, but you have to write the sonnet yourself. What you say is completely up to you.
> Madeleine L'Engle, *A Wrinkle in Time*, 1962

LIFELONG LEARNING

Librarians work in their own intellectual playgrounds. We are a people who love to learn everything about everything. In fact, a particular discipline would be too confining for librarians, because we see the patterns in knowledge, and we delight in helping students build understanding from cross-disciplinary connections. We strive for excellence, as a habit of our actions, by continuing to find new methods to serve our students in deeper and more authentic ways.

> I am still learning.
> Michelangelo, Italian Renaissance painter, sculptor, poet, and engineer, 1475–1564

"Library as Place"

"Library as place" has been a construct in U.S. society since we were a young democratic country. The public library provides opportunities for our citizens to become informed in a local, familiar, community environment that serves their specific demographic. The school

> It's still a beautiful place in the library.
> ALA Poster, circa 1990

library program, as a microcosm, seeks to develop library habits in our youngest of citizens. Collaboration with the public library serves to enhance both libraries' program offerings. Virtual libraries have resources and community spaces for library users. As "library as place" transforms from the physical library to both physical and virtual spaces, it seems timely to discuss the notion of the concept of library as an intellectual concept that provides for the life of the mind, by making informed decisions about habits of information behavior. This place is within us. Library users have strategies and habits that guide their use of library resources and programming. The community center that exists will continue to evolve but should not be considered to be the sole heir to the library concept. As students search online, we want library dispositions to guide their information behaviors. As students develop into lifelong learners, we believe that the library as a concept is one that will continue to enrich their lives with meaning and fulfillment.

QUESTIONS AND ANSWERS ABOUT PROFESSIONAL ETHICS

1. I was a classroom teacher before I went into the school library. I never thought about professional ethics as a teacher; I just wanted to be a good teacher to every one of my students. Now that the concept of professional ethics is raised, it strikes me as ironic that I am no longer considered a professional, even though I needed to take graduate courses in school librarianship and add to my education credentials. Just as when I was a teacher, can't I just get through each day and take the measure of my success from my impact on student learning?

   Agreed, school librarians are in a tricky position. We straddle both the library and information science field and the education field, and, in the process, we are looked down upon by both. Other librarians seem to have distain for us, and teachers feel that either we wanted to get out of the classroom or are not equal to them as teachers. Administrators don't seem to know where to weigh in on the issue. The fact remains that librarianship is a profession replete with values, standards, and ethics and that school librarianship is a subset within that profession. We share the values of librarians and have national standards that guide our commitment to our learning communities. Our professional ethics are a blend of both education and library ethics and are actuated each day through practical applications in our interactions with students and teachers. We all need to continue to fine-tune our practice by reminding ourselves that there are ethics that guide the many decisions we face as school librarians.

2. In my desire to have good working relationships with my teachers, I offer my services as a top-notch researcher to those who are taking graduate courses. Some teachers take advantage of what I consider to be a generous offer, and I find myself in a bad situation when they want more than I want to deliver. Maybe this does not come under the professional ethics banner, but is there a limit to the service orientation that we have in our field? How do I achieve the right balance?

You probably offer yourself to friends and colleagues, and sometimes that offer is abused, so you may regret that you were so generous. The same holds true in this situation.

What you are doing sounds like it is more in your nature as a compassionate person than as a professional. In that regard, you cannot exactly point at our ethics and say, "They made me do it," but rather take responsibility for your own actions. It sounds like it would be beneficial to you to put limits on your offer of assistance so that it does not get out of hand. And also consider the lengths you might go to help someone do his or her research. Even your teachers are students, and it does not help them to do their research for them. Give guidance, advice, and let them decide how far they want to take their research. Their academic librarians at their universities will step in as you step out; their public librarians will follow through on interlibrary loan; let other librarians serving your teachers as patrons carry some of the service orientation as well.

READ MORE ABOUT PROFESSIONAL ETHICS

Adams, H. R. 2007. The age of the patron: Privacy for middle and high school students. *School Library Media Activities Monthly* 23(8): 38.

The ethical role of privacy for middle and high school students is clearly addressed in this short article by Adams. She explains that a school librarian must have background knowledge of state and national laws on minors' privacy before being able to address the students. This knowledge, combined with the Code of Ethics of the American Library Association and common sense for student welfare, will assure a solid foundation. The reader is given five examples of how to obtain an overdue library book from a student without violating his or her privacy. The conclusion reminds school librarians that, although teens want privacy, they must be taught how to protect it online.

Butler, R. P. 2005. The school librarian and on-the-job ethics. *Knowledge Quest* 33(5): 33–34.

This article begins by giving four very common examples of ethical concerns that may arise in a library media center. The concerns deal with equitable access, intellectual freedom, copyright, and privacy. Butler explains each dilemma and connects its solution to *Information Power* information literacy standards 7 and 8 and/or the Bill of Rights.

Gorman, M. 2000. *Our enduring values: Librarianship in the 21st century.* Chicago: American Library Association.

Gorman grounds the core values of librarianship in historical and professional context while exploring challenges that lay ahead in the 21st century. Values of service and stewardship are in great transition and also enduring; intellectual freedom, privacy, and democracy never felt more fundamental to our profession than they do at this moment in time.

Simpson, C. 2003. *Ethics in school librarianship: A reader.* Worthington, OH: Linworth.

Simpson introduces the importance of professional ethics, and respected contributors explore topics that include collection development; school library access; confidentiality, use of technology; intellectual freedom; intellectual property; administration; Internet use; and professional relationships. Discussion questions help further the readers' thinking on each topic.

CONNECTING TO 21ST-CENTURY LEARNERS

The *AASL Standards for the 21st-Century Learner* were written, as stated, for the learner. That learner might be a student or teacher, child or adult. Certainly every school librarian is a 21st-century learner, and the connections to the standards in every other chapter highlight the ways in which we model the learner dispositions to help our students observe our thinking and learning behaviors and actions. The connection to the standards with professional ethics relates more specifically to the Common Beliefs that introduce the standards. The following nine beliefs summarize our values, ethics, and responsibilities as school librarians:

- Reading is a window to the world
- Inquiry provides a framework for learning
- Ethical behavior in the use of information must be taught
- Technology skills are crucial for future employment needs
- Equitable access is a key component for education
- The definition of information literacy has become more complex as resources and technologies have changed
- The continuing expansion of information demands that all individuals acquire the thinking skills that will enable them to learn on their own
- Learning has a social context
- School libraries are essential to the development learning skills

Our professional ethics guide our behavior with all members of our learning community in the same way that our belief system guides our practice with learners. Without this foundation of underlying assumptions, our standards would not have the power to transform learners through their school library experiences. Take time to study and discuss the Common Beliefs. Think about them as guiding principles as you interpret the learner standards for your students in your school. This will be a true act of service to your learning community and will also give you a strong base to continue to inform and improve your practice.

DISPOSITIONAL PROMPTS ABOUT PROFESSIONAL ETHICS

1. This year I have decided to focus on fostering a climate of literacy among the adults in the school learning community. I want to demonstrate to the children that the parents, teachers, administration, and staff are readers and that their lives are enriched by reading. There is only one problem. They aren't, and it isn't. But I still feel strongly about this, and I think I feel correct in calling this a disposition. I am modeling the Dispositions in Action for students in the fourth standard "pursuing personal and aesthetic growth." But it is like throwing a party and no one comes. Should I stick to my gut feeling, or read the writing on the wall?

2. I am insistent about following copyright laws, and the photocopier that is in the library media center has become a battleground. Teachers are trying to come in when I am out of the library so that they can copy anything regardless of copyright. Long ago they stopped asking me to copy VHS onto DVDs for them, but they still do not truly understand the issue. And yes, these are the same teachers whose students are found plagiarizing, and they don't know what to do about it. Again, do I continue to be a copyright vigilante, or do I soften my grip to go along to get along?

Epilogue

"Excuse me, sorry to bother you, but are you Mrs. J., Mrs. Janceski?"

"Yes, I'm Donna Janceski, but I'm sorry, you'll have to remind me."

"I can't believe you are here! I'm Reggie, Reggie Lorenz, from LHS. I was in your English class."

"Tennis, right?"

"Yeah, how did you remember that?"

"I supervised a tournament once when you were playing during the year you were my student. How *are* you, Reggie?"

"I'm fine, thanks. I'm just so surprised to see you here, Mrs. J. What are you doing at a school librarians' conference?"

"I am the librarian at Lincoln now. This is my seventh year. What are you doing these days, Reggie, do you have a family? Wait a minute, tell me what *you* are doing here?"

"You won't believe this, but I am a librarian too, at Jefferson Middle School in Evansville. And I'm still single, Mrs. J. Anyway, I was in the district tech department, and I moved into the middle school library last year.

Oh, I'm sorry. Mrs. Janceski, this is Lisa Taylor. I just met Lisa in the last workshop I went to this morning. Lisa, this is Mrs. Janceski, my former English teacher from Lincoln High School in Williamsport."

"Hi Lisa, nice to meet you, call me Donna. And that goes for you too, Reggie."

"Hi Donna, it's nice to meet you too. Listen, do you two want to reminisce? Should I leave you alone?"

"No way, let's just grab our box lunches and sit down over there. Mrs. J., I mean Donna, Lisa is the librarian over at Washington Elementary in Springfield. We both went to a workshop called "Reading and Literacy in the Digital Age." We just met by sitting near each other and then getting grouped together at the same round table in the workshop. What session did you go to this morning?"

"Please join us, Lisa. I'll save these seats; you two pick up the boxes. Reggie, just find a turkey or ham sandwich for me and a bottle of water, thanks. Oh, I went to a session on information literacy and the benchmarks and all that, rolled up together with our state learning standards. It was okay, not very exciting stuff.
So, Lisa, how long have you been at Washington?"

"This is my fourth year. I was a middle school science teacher, but that didn't work out. I like working in schools though, so I thought that I would just try another angle. I like the library, I absolutely love my students, I am trying to learn my job, but I'll tell you, working with the teachers is my biggest challenge."

"Really? How so?"

"I don't want to sound ungrateful. I have a really supportive principal, and I know that a lot of school librarians cannot say that, but if I don't start taking her advice, she might not keep thinking so much of me. You know, I "have leadership potential." I am hoping that this year will be my breakout year. That's really why I'm here. I have never gone to a school library conference before, but I heard about it from a librarian at school near mine. Dr. Kelly, my principal, thought it would be good for me to "network," and she approved it."

"This is my first one too, of course, 'cause last year was my first year in the library. I don't know, I think the library job has so many moving parts to it. In my mind, the whole middle school thing has got to be about the kids. Period. We have teachers who think that it is all about learning the content of their subject, no offense Lisa, and they wonder what is wrong with the kids when they can't learn from them, and I think they have it all wrong. I just smile and listen to them complain, and let it go in one ear and out the other. Every middle schooler everywhere is hurting or is insecure or is questioning or is suffering from too much attention or too little attention from parents or someone or something, I don't care if they have money or not. I think that they all have needs that get in the way of their learning. It is amazing that any learning goes on at all, and it is amazing to me that there are teachers who don't get that—at all."

"So how do you like it in the library compared to the tech job, Reggie? Can you spend the kind of time with the kids that you would like to?"

"Well, I had this one experience last year with this little guy who needed a place to hang, Abir. I'll tell you just one story, and I think you'll understand.

So, some of our teachers have all these multicultural units that they think make all the kids feel good about their heritage and everything. I'm not saying they are all bad but—let me tell you what happened. So Abir is really upset after school, and it turns out that he had to research the meaning of his name in the computer lab that day. Abir said that he didn't think that he was going to find anything. And, you know, I figure some kids tease him about his name. The kids used all these names sites for the assignment, and it turns out that Abir has a seriously unique name because it has meaning in both Arabic and Hebrew. Mr. Bilquist, the teacher, went nuts loving it, thinking this assignment was the greatest thing, and, at the same time, Abir felt sick about it. He just didn't know if he should like that or not, if it was a good thing or a bad thing, and he felt queasy. Abir said that Mr. Bilquist got mad at him when he did not look happy and said that most people would like to learn that their names have meaning in two "conflicting cultures," that is was some sign of unity or something. Man, he looked terrible when he was telling me about it. I didn't know if I should talk to Bilquist about Abir, but I decided to hold off. And Abir didn't know if he should tell anyone at home about it or keep it a secret.

Sorry, it became a long story, but even telling you about it, I can't believe how much Abir had an impact on me last year. And I was really mad at first when the AP saddled me with him. Now I think I'll always remember him. I learned a lot about how I want to handle my position and also just about how much these kids have going on. I know he is an extreme case maybe, but still."

"Reggie, I never thought about a situation like that. I worked with two teachers who had students research their nations. I wonder how Abir would feel about that. Really, thanks for telling us about him. I'll keep that in mind. I'm so glad you told us that story.

So, anyway, this is my first time here too. I knew about these conferences, but I was not interested in going to anything outside of my school. I decided, after working with some teachers last year, that I should figure out some things about what the school library should offer our students. But I will be honest. My youngest daughter is a freshman in college this year. I think that, for the last six years, I was in a holding pattern while the girls were going through their teens and I was learning a new job—just the way the last librarian did her job—I just followed her lead. I am pretty good about knowing my limits and my personal life had to take priority.

Now that the girls are launched and Ray and I are empty-nesters, I feel this new freedom to learn and think about my professional life. So I want to start to write some little grants and to think about the library collection. I really do love Lincoln and want to do right by the students there. I hate the thought that I am out of step with what our students need. I mean, everything is fine and all, but it's just so status quo. And all of a sudden, I don't think that's okay. I hardly recognize myself when I say that, but that's how I feel now. I need to punch up my game. Maybe when you get older, you feel less fear of failure. For whatever reason, I'm ready to try some things and see if they fly. I don't have too far to fall because I have not risked anything yet anyway."

"Do you have ideas for grants that you want to write?"

"I worked with this one new English teacher last year, Stephanie. She wanted "edgy" books, and I kind of poo-pooed the whole idea and handed it off to the youth services librarian at the public library. Now I am thinking that it would be fun to put Stephanie together with Marta, who teaches world history, to look at censorship around the world. It's just an idea. We could tie it into Banned Books Week maybe. Anyway, this whole grants thing is kind of scary but could be fun, and I think it will help me look at the library program more critically, I guess. I don't know. I should be able to write the proposals, because I was an English teacher, but I don't know all the rest of what goes into it. I have talked to some really veteran school librarians; some of them have never written a grant and are petrified of the idea, and others do it all the time; some proposals are funded, some are not, but they think that it is a good way to look at things. When I was in grad school, they really encouraged the whole grant idea, but we were all so overwhelmed at the time I don't think anyone was really listening when they taught us how to look for grants.

"I think it's great that you have this new burst of energy. Talk about overwhelmed, I am just overwhelmed because every time I try to talk to the teachers, it is a complete and total disaster. They want to drop their kids at the library and run as fast as they can to their prep periods. That's life in the elementary school library lane. Even the teachers who are my friends act the same way. I don't get it. So, I'm here to soak up the support from each other and "network" quote unquote. I thought I'd go to the collaboration workshop this afternoon. I really want to see if there is a way I could learn to talk to teachers about this reading group idea I have. Reggie, what are you going to do after lunch?"

"I might just go to see the exhibits to see the vendors and the new books. I am looking at some series nonfiction from one of the publishers—or there are two sessions I might go to. One is on preventing dropping out, which I think should be talked about at the middle school level, but I'm surprised to see a session on it at a school library conference, or I'll go to the one about booktalks—that is my absolute worst thing that I do."

"Well, at least we came, and we're all learning new things, and meeting you two is great. This lunch has made it worth the drive for me. It is like our own little buddy system—like when I used to have clinical hours in labs all the time in college—you would never think of working alone. Anyway, thanks so much for inviting me to have lunch with you."

"I couldn't agree with you more, Lisa. So I have a little idea. What do you think about us meeting at some other school library conferences and things? We could e-mail and let each other know about what's going on around the state and plan to meet at them. I'll offer to start the e-mail group. What do you think Reggie?"

"Sounds good to me. Maybe we'll even go to something national one of these days if it is in our part of the country. Okay, you two have convinced me that I need to stretch. I can't believe it, but I'm going to the booktalking session! They better not ask me to say anything. I don't know any books. Anyway, here's my e-mail address. This has been great."

"Let me check my map here: the collaboration workshop is in the Capitol Room upstairs. I am so happy that we all met up. Here's my e-mail address,

Donna. Thanks for offering to start it off for us. We can have our own mini-e-mail group. I love it. Just the right size. Okay, hope to see you both again, great meeting you."

"Alright, time to go. Reggie, you picked up my lunch, so I will clear it for us. I'm bringing my cookie as a pick-me-up for later. Wish me luck. I am going to the grant writing workshop. I hope they don't have us doing anything there today—it will be too much like taking a test. Bye Reggie, it is so so good to see you again. Lisa, it was lovely meeting you. Let's stay in touch. I'll plan on sending out the e-mail next week. Okay, bye for now."

Appendix

The AASL *Standards for the 21st-Century Learner* and the Dispositions in Action

STANDARD 1: INQUIRE, THINK CRITICALLY, AND GAIN KNOWLEDGE.

Dispositions in Action for Standard 1

1.2.1   Display initiative and engagement by posing questions and investigating the answers beyond the collection of superficial facts.

1.2.2   Demonstrate confidence and self-direction by making independent choices in the selection of resources and information.

1.2.3   Demonstrate creativity by using multiple resources and formats.

1.2.4   Maintain a critical stance by questioning the validity and accuracy of all information.

1.2.5   Demonstrate adaptability by changing the inquiry focus, questions, resources, or strategies when necessary to achieve success.

1.2.6   Display emotional resiliency by persisting in information searching despite challenges.

1.2.7   Display persistence by continuing to pursue information to gain a broad perspective.

STANDARD 2: DRAW CONCLUSIONS, MAKE INFORMED DECISIONS, APPLY KNOWLEDGE TO NEW SITUATIONS, AND CREATE NEW KNOWLEDGE.

Dispositions in Action for Standard 2

2.2.1   Demonstrate flexibility in the use of resources by adapting information strategies to each specific resource and by seeking additional resources when clear conclusions cannot be drawn.

2.2.2   Use both divergent and convergent thinking to formulate alternative conclusions and test them against the evidence.

2.2.3   Employ a critical stance in drawing conclusions by demonstrating that the pattern of evidence leads to a discussion or conclusion.

2.2.4   Demonstrate personal productivity by completing products to express learning.

STANDARD 3: SHARE KNOWLEDGE AND PARTICIPATE ETHICALLY AND PRODUCTIVELY AS MEMBERS OF OUR DEMOCRATIC SOCIETY.

Dispositions in Action for Standard 3

3.2.1   Demonstrate leadership and confidence by presenting ideas to others in both formal and informal situations.

3.2.2   Show social responsibility by participating actively with others in learning situations and by contributing questions and ideas during group discussions.

3.2.3   Demonstrate teamwork by working productively with others.

STANDARD 4: PURSUE PERSONAL AND AESTHETIC GROWTH.

Dispositions in Action for Standard 4

4.2.1   Display curiosity by pursuing interests through multiple resources.

4.2.2   Demonstrate motivation by seeking information to answer personal questions and interests, trying a variety of formats and genres, and displaying a willingness to go beyond academic requirements.

4.2.3   Maintain openness to new ideas by considering divergent opinions, changing opinions or conclusions when evidence supports the change, and seeking information about new ideas encountered through academic or personal experiences.

4.2.4   Show an appreciation for literature by electing to read for pleasure and expressing an interest in various literary genres.

Quotations Bibliography

As we indicated in our Introduction, "the reader will be treated to quotes from literature for all ages, words of wisdom and folly." We offer this bibliography as a clue into our sources. We pulled and pondered, clipped and cited. Nevertheless, we recognize that some quotes require more research to document their origins fully. Hopefully, we will set you on a path of discovery as we invite you to go forth and research at will.

Alex-Lute, M. 2001. *Quotation index to children's literature*. Englewood, CO: Libraries Unlimited.

American Library Association. Notable Quotes. 2009. http://www.ala.org/Template.cfm ?Section=bbwlinks&Template=/ContentManagement/ContentDisplay.cfm&Conten tID=60516.

Benardete, D., ed. 1961. *Mark Twain: Wit and wisecracks*. NY: Peter Pauper Press.

Brainy Quote. http://www.brainyquote.com.

Byrne, R. 2006. *The 2,548 best things anybody ever said*. NY: Simon & Schuster.

Calaprice, A., ed. 2002. *Dear Professor Einstein: Albert Einstein's letters to and from children*. NY: Barnes & Noble.

Carroll, L. 1871. *Through the looking-glass*. London: Macmillan.

Cleary, B. 1983. *Dear Mr. Henshaw*. NY: HarperCollins.

DePree, M. 1992. *Leadership jazz*. NY: Dell.

Gash, A. 1999. *What the doormouse said*. Chapel Hill, NC: Algonquin Books.

Henderson, N., B. Benard, and N. Sharp-Light., eds. 2000. *Schoolwide approaches for fostering resiliency*. San Diego: Resiliency in Action.

Keller, H. 1905. *The story of my life*. NY: Doubleday.

Krumgold, J. 1959. *Onion John*. NY: Crowell.

L'Engle, M. 1962. *A wrinkle in time*. NY: Farrar Straus Giroux.

Milne, A. A. 1926. *Winnie-the-Pooh*. NY: Dutton.

Martin, Jr., B. and Archambault, J. 1989. *Chicka chicka boom boom*. NY: Simon & Schuster.

Peter, L. J. 1977. *Peter's quotations: Ideas for our time*. NY: Morrow.

Piper, W. 1930. *The little engine that could.* NY: Platt & Munk.

The Quotations Page. http://www.quotationspage.com.

Rochman, H. 1993. *Against borders: Promoting books for a multicultural world.* Chicago: American Library Association.

Schrage, M. 1990. *No more teams! Mastering the dynamics of creative collaboration.* NY: Doubleday.

Sierra, J. 2004. *Wild about books.* New York: Alfred A. Knopf.

ThinkExist. http://thinkexist.com/quotations/literature.

U.S. Department of Education, National Center for Education Statistics. 2004. *The status of public and private school library media centers in the United States, 1999–2000.* Washington, DC: U.S. Government Printing Office.

White, E. B. 1952. *Charlotte's web.* NY: HarperCollins.

About the Authors and Contributors

Gail Bush, PhD, is a professor in the Reading and Language Department at National-Louis University in Chicago, IL. She is director of the Center for Teaching through Children's Books (along with Dr. Junko Yokota) and director of the School Library Program. Dr. Bush has edited *The Best of KQ: School Libraries in Action: Civil Engagement, Social Justice, and Equity* (2009, AASL) and written *Every Student Reads* (2005, AASL) and *The School Buddy System: The Practice of Collaboration* (2003, ALA Editions).

Jami Biles Jones, PhD, is an assistant professor in the Department of Library Science at East Carolina University in Greenville, NC. In 2002, Dr. Jones received National Board Certification in Early Childhood/Young Adult Media. Dr. Jones has written *The Power of the Media Specialist to Improve Academic Achievement and Strengthen At-risk Youth* (with Alana M. Zambone) (2008, Linworth), *Bouncing Back: Dealing with the Stuff Life Throws at You* (2007, Franklin Watts), and *Helping Teens Cope: Resources for School Library Media Specialists and Other Youth Workers* (2003, Linworth).

Contributor Information

Gail K. Dickinson, PhD, is an associate professor of library science at Old Dominion University in Norfolk, VA. Dr. Dickinson is the author of *Achieving National Board Certification for School Library Media Specialists* (2006, ALA) among other titles and editorial director of *LMC: Library Media Connections*.

Carrie Gardner, PhD, is an assistant professor in the Department of Library Science and Instructional Technology at Kutztown University in Kutztown Pennsylvania. She is a member of the ALA Intellectual Freedom Committee and the Freedom to Read Foundation Board of Trustees.

Theodore R. Sizer, PhD, was professor emeritus, Brown University, and visiting professor, Harvard and Brandeis universities, and founder and chairman emeritus of the Coalition of Essential Schools. Dr. Sizer was author of many articles, chapters, and books on all aspects of U.S. educational reform, most notably the *Horace* trilogy, which is discussed in the Foreword to this book.

Index

Page numbers followed by an italicized *f* indicate figures.